KRISTEN PARKER

The Warden Who Loved the Stars

Contents

1 The Silent Keeper   1

2 A Shifting Light   12

3 Forbidden Meeting   23

4 The Searing Darkness   34

5 The Heart of the Tower   45

6 The Price of Sacrifice   55

7 The Rift of Trust   66

8 The Abyss Beckons   77

9 The Shattered Realm   89

10 The Battle of Hearts   100

11 The Warden's Choice   111

12 The Star's Last Breath   121

13 A Celestial Rebirth   132

14 Echoes in the Night Sky   142

15 The Warden's Legacy   152

16 Whispers of the Heart   163

17 The New Dawn   172

18 The End of Eternity   182

19 Between the Ember and the Tide   193

20 Forever Bound   202

One

The Silent Keeper

I solde stood at the edge of the vast celestial tower, her eyes fixed on the endless expanse of stars above. The night sky stretched infinitely, a tapestry of glowing specks of light that twinkled like diamonds in the inky void. The stars, though beautiful, were far more than mere celestial bodies. They were living beings—each one a guardian in its own right, a force of nature, an ancient spirit that carried the weight of the universe within its core.

Her breath was steady as she gazed up at the stars, her mind calm and alert. As the Warden, she had sworn an oath to protect them, to guard them against the creeping darkness that threatened to engulf everything. The stars were the keepers of balance, the foundation of the universe, and it was her responsibility to ensure they remained unharmed, to guard them against the shadow that always lurked at the edges, threatening to extinguish their light.

The celestial tower, where she had spent countless years in solitude, was her watchtower. It was a place that stretched high above the clouds, where the sky opened up before her like an endless ocean of stars. She had never wavered in her duty. For centuries, she had stood alone, watching, waiting, the guardian of the light. But tonight, something was different. Something in the air felt heavy, like the calm before a storm.

Isolde's fingers clenched around the cold railing of the tower as she leaned forward, her heart quickening with a sudden, inexplicable unease. She had felt it earlier that day, a subtle disturbance in the flow of the stars, a flicker of something unnatural. But she had dismissed it, convinced it was nothing more than a fleeting moment. Now, as she stood at the edge of the tower, that feeling was undeniable.

The stars shifted above her, their light pulsing with a rhythm that was almost hypnotic. But one of them, just one, was flickering—a faint shadow moving across the brilliance of its light, like a storm cloud obscuring the glow of the moon.

Isolde's breath caught in her throat. She had never seen anything like this before. No star had ever faltered in such a way. The balance, the delicate harmony that kept the universe in place, was at risk.

Her eyes narrowed, focusing on the flickering star. It was not just any star, she realized. It was Lior, the most radiant of them all—his light burned brighter than any other, his form so striking that it almost made her breath catch every time she gazed upon it. Lior had always been a constant, a steady beacon in the night sky. He was the star of the East, the brightest in the constellation that marked the beginning of the universe's cycles. His light was pure, unwavering.

But tonight, it flickered. The light was dimming.

Isolde's heart raced. She had never allowed herself to feel this way before. She had always been the Keeper, the guardian of these celestial beings, but now, standing at the edge of the tower, something inside her shifted. There was an undeniable pull toward Lior, a magnetic force drawing her toward him—an attraction she had never experienced. It was as if his light called to her in a way that no other star had.

She clenched her jaw and forced herself to step back from the railing. Her duty was clear. She couldn't afford to let her emotions cloud her judgment. Her responsibility was to protect the stars, not to become entangled in their mysteries. But the pull was there, as strong as the gravitational force between two celestial bodies, and she could feel it deep in her chest, in the very marrow of her bones.

As the Warden, she had been trained to see the stars as nothing more than beacons of light, symbols of the cosmic balance. But Lior was different. There was something in his presence, something in the way he shimmered in the sky, that made him seem almost… alive. Not just alive in the way that all stars were, but alive in a way that felt personal, as if he were meant to be something more than a distant force.

She had never allowed herself to think about the stars in such a way before. But now, as she gazed up at him, she wondered—was there a part of her heart that longed to know him beyond her duty? Was there a part of her that yearned for something more?

The sound of soft footsteps behind her snapped Isolde back to the present. She turned quickly, her heart still hammering in her chest, to find her fellow warden, Alaric, standing just inside the archway of the tower.

"Warden Isolde," Alaric greeted her in his usual measured

tone. He was a tall man, his silver hair glinting in the faint starlight that filtered into the tower. His sharp features were set in an expression of calm determination, though there was something unreadable in his eyes.

"I've felt it, too," Alaric said, his voice low but carrying across the stillness of the night. "Lior… his light is dimming. We've never seen anything like this before."

Isolde turned her gaze back to Lior, her stomach sinking. "What does it mean?" she asked, her voice strained. "Why is this happening? Is there something we missed?"

Alaric's gaze flickered to the sky, his brows furrowing. "The stars are not meant to falter," he said quietly. "There are forces that we have long kept at bay—forces beyond our understanding. It could be that this is the beginning of something we can't control."

Isolde's pulse quickened as she stared at Lior's fading light. The shadows that surrounded him seemed to grow darker, swirling around him like a cloud of smoke that threatened to suffocate his radiance. She felt it deep in her chest—the tightening of her breath, the ache in her bones. The balance was shifting. The stars were beginning to fall into chaos.

"We need to do something," she whispered, her fingers tightening around the railing. "If we don't act now, Lior might…"

"Don't say it," Alaric interrupted sharply. "We've trained for this. We will protect the stars."

But even as he said the words, Isolde could see the fear in his eyes. They both knew that their training, their years of service, might not be enough this time. This was different. Lior was different.

For a long moment, the two wardens stood in silence, the

gravity of the situation settling over them like a blanket of cold dread. Then, Isolde spoke, her voice soft but filled with determination.

"I need to go to him," she said, her gaze fixed firmly on Lior's flickering light. "I need to find out what's causing this. I need to understand what's happening to him."

Alaric's expression shifted, a flicker of surprise crossing his face. "You cannot," he warned. "You know the rules, Isolde. The stars are not to be approached. We protect them from afar, but we never get too close."

"I don't care about the rules," she replied fiercely, her voice rising. "This is different. I can't stand here and do nothing while he suffers."

For the first time, Alaric hesitated. He glanced toward the sky, then back at her, his expression troubled. "You know the consequences, Isolde. If you get too close, if you intervene…"

She didn't need him to finish the sentence. They both knew that the price for getting too close to the stars was steep. The wardens had always been warned that any connection with the celestial beings—any emotional entanglement—could result in the loss of their own humanity. Once bound to a star, a warden could lose everything: their memories, their sense of self, their very soul.

Isolde's heart thudded in her chest as she weighed the decision. She knew what she was about to do was reckless, dangerous, forbidden. But she couldn't let Lior fade away without trying to save him. She couldn't stand by while the universe, the very thing she had sworn to protect, crumbled in front of her.

"I'm going," she said, her voice steady now. "And you can't stop me."

Alaric's eyes darkened, and for a moment, she saw the weight of his own doubts reflected there. But in the end, he nodded. "I'll prepare the transport," he said quietly. "But you'll have to face the consequences, Isolde. Whatever happens… you'll be on your own."

With that, he turned and disappeared into the depths of the tower, leaving Isolde alone with her thoughts. She turned back to the stars, her heart racing. Lior's light flickered once more, a flash of brilliance that seemed to waver in the darkness.

The universe was calling. And this time, Isolde would answer.

She had no idea what awaited her. No idea what consequences her actions would bring. But she couldn't ignore the pull she felt toward him—the pull that had grown stronger than any duty, any oath.

She would save him. Even if it cost her everything.

The wind picked up as Isolde stood at the edge of the tower, the faint hum of celestial magic coursing through her veins, amplifying the intensity of her emotions. She could feel the weight of the decision pressing on her chest, but the call to Lior—the unseen thread that bound her heart to his—was undeniable. Her body was no longer her own, it seemed. She could hear the stars, feel their vibrations as if they were an extension of her. But it was Lior's light, flickering weakly against the growing darkness, that consumed her every thought.

Alaric's warning echoed in her mind. *You'll be on your own.* But even as those words rang in her ears, they did nothing to quell the burning determination inside her. She had been trained to guard, to watch, to remain silent in her duty. But now, for the first time in her long service, she felt the walls of her solitude crack. She was not just the Warden anymore; she was something more—something deeply entwined with the stars themselves.

As she moved toward the ancient archway that led to the transport room, her steps seemed to quicken with each breath she took. Every part of her body knew what she was about to do was dangerous. But the force pulling her toward Lior was stronger than any rule, any regulation. And the more she tried to ignore it, the more it grew—until it was the only thing she could feel.

The transport room was dimly lit, filled with the quiet hum of celestial energy. Alaric was already there, his expression as unreadable as ever, his hands adjusting the glowing crystal that powered the dimensional gate. He didn't say a word when she entered, but his eyes lingered on her with an emotion she couldn't quite place—concern, perhaps, or perhaps a quiet resignation.

"I've prepared the gate," he said, his voice calm, but Isolde could hear the underlying tension. He didn't approve of her decision, but he wasn't stopping her either.

"Thank you," she replied softly, her throat tight with the weight of the moment.

Alaric didn't respond. He just nodded, stepping aside, allowing her to step closer to the swirling vortex of energy that now pulsed in front of her. It shimmered with the light of a thousand stars, the patterns of space and time folding around it like a living thing. The gates were designed to traverse the vast reaches of the cosmos, a tool only for the Wardens when they were called upon by the celestial order. It would take her to Lior—directly to the heart of the realm where the stars resided.

Without a second thought, Isolde stepped into the portal.

The world around her shattered into light and sound, and for a brief moment, her senses were overwhelmed. Time and space bent around her, disorienting and unrelenting, as the celestial fabric tore apart and reformed. She had never traveled so far before, had never ventured so close to the very beings she had sworn to protect. But as she tumbled through the darkness, her heart still beat, steady and determined.

The portal spit her out with a sudden, violent jolt, throwing her into the void of space. She tumbled and caught herself, instinctively drawing on the magic that flowed through her veins. It was different here—this place was not the same as the solid ground she had known. Here, she was weightless, suspended among the stars themselves, surrounded by an abyss of darkness and light, where the boundaries between the two seemed to blur.

The light she sought was just ahead—Lior. His radiant form flickered, as though struggling to hold onto its brilliance in the face of something dark and invasive. Her pulse quickened, and she reached out toward him, her arms stretched wide, her heart pounding in her chest.

"Lior!" she called out, her voice lost in the void, but she knew he could hear her. She had to believe that. He was fading, but she couldn't let him slip away. Not now.

A flicker of light pulsed back, and then—there he was. Lior's form, beautiful and luminous, yet dimming as if he were trapped in an inescapable storm. His light was flickering more erratically now, shadows swirling around him, tendrils of dark magic that seemed to choke the very air around them.

"Isolde..." Lior's voice was soft, his tone a mixture of pain and relief, as though he had been waiting for her, expecting her to come. But there was something in his eyes—a distant, unfocused look, as though he could no longer hold onto his form fully. "You shouldn't have come…"

"I had to," she said, her voice trembling as she floated closer to him. "I couldn't stand by and watch you fade. What is happening to you?"

He shuddered, his light flickering once more before settling into a steady pulse, though still much dimmer than it should have been. "There is a darkness… an ancient curse," Lior whispered, his voice barely audible. "It's not just the shadows that you see. It's an attack on my very being… on the stars themselves."

Isolde's heart lurched, and she reached out, her fingers brushing against his ethereal form. The warmth of his glow was still there, but it was growing weaker, threatened by something far more sinister. She had always known the stars had their own dangers, but never before had she witnessed one so vulnerable, so fragile.

"Tell me what to do," she whispered urgently. "I'll do anything. Just—just tell me how to save you."

Lior's gaze softened, and there was a tenderness in his eyes that cut through the fear threatening to rise within her. "You can't save me," he said gently. "The curse has already begun. It is not something that can be undone. I am fading, Isolde. And with me, the balance of the universe will fall."

"No," she said, shaking her head, as if by refusing to acknowledge the truth, she could defy it. "There must be another way. You've always been the brightest. You've always been the protector. You can't just vanish."

The light around him dimmed further, but his voice remained calm, as though he had already accepted his fate. "I am not just a star, Isolde. I am the last of a line of celestial guardians. My light is the anchor that holds the balance, but without it—without me—the universe will crumble."

Her breath caught in her throat, the weight of his words sinking in. She had come to save him, but the reality was much worse than she had imagined. The fate of the universe itself was tied to Lior. If he died, so too would the stars. The very fabric of space would begin to unravel, and with it, everything they had ever known would cease to exist.

"No," Isolde whispered again, her voice trembling with both fear and sorrow. She could feel the weight of his presence, the immensity of his being, even in his weakened state. His power was greater than she had ever realized, and to lose him meant losing everything.

"I cannot change what is already in motion," Lior said, his voice quieter now, like the fading whisper of a dying wind. "But you can. You, Isolde. You are the Warden. You can protect the stars—*all* the stars—by becoming one with them."

The words struck her like lightning. "What do you mean?" she asked, confusion lacing her voice. "How can I protect them? I am just a keeper."

Lior's glow brightened slightly, as though he were mustering the last of his strength. "The stars are not mere lights in the sky. We are life. We are the force that keeps this universe alive. To protect the stars, you must become a part of them. You must… sacrifice yourself."

A cold shiver ran down Isolde's spine. "Sacrifice myself?" she echoed, her mind reeling. "But… how? And why?"

Lior's eyes met hers, filled with a sadness she could barely comprehend. "The bond between the stars and their wardens is stronger than you know. But to save the stars, to restore the balance, you must become the light. You must take my place."

The realization hit her like a physical blow. Her heart twisted painfully as she grasped the enormity of what he was asking her to do. She would give up everything—her very essence, her humanity, to save him, to save them all.

"I can't," she whispered, shaking her head. "I can't lose myself."

"You won't lose yourself," Lior said, his voice soft and tender. "You will be reborn, a part of the stars, a part of everything. Your essence will be woven into the fabric of the universe. You will carry me with you, always."

The decision lay before her, heavy as the stars themselves. To save him—to save everything—she would have to give up her life as she knew it. But could she let go of everything she had ever been? Could she step into the unknown, become something greater than herself, for the sake of the stars, for the sake of the universe?

Tears blurred her vision as she reached out toward Lior. Her fingers brushed against his fading light, and in that moment, she knew what she had to do.

The darkness was encroaching, and the stars were dimming. Isolde had to choose—her love for Lior, or the sacrifice that could save everything.

And as she stepped toward him, ready to embrace her fate, she knew that no matter the cost, she would do it. For the stars. For Lior. For the universe.

With a final, steadying breath, she whispered, "I will save it.

Two

A Shifting Light

The nights grew longer, and with each passing evening, Isolde's gaze returned to the darkened sky where Lior's light flickered like the dying embers of a once-brilliant fire. She could feel it deep within her—his struggle, the shadow creeping along the edges of his light. The quiet hum of celestial magic vibrated in her bones as she stood at the tower's edge, her eyes fixed on the wavering star. It was a pull she couldn't explain, a connection deeper than anything she had ever known. She was the warden of the stars, but Lior… Lior had become something else. Something dangerous.

Every time she looked at him, she felt something stir inside her—something fragile, something forbidden. The stars were her duty. They were not to be touched, not to be loved, not to be saved with personal attachment. The wardens had always been taught to remain detached, to keep their hearts separate from their charge. It was the only way to maintain the balance.

But with Lior's light flickering in the distance, her heart beat to a rhythm she could not control.

She closed her eyes, her breath catching as the darkness around her seemed to deepen. As though on cue, the images began to flood her mind—images of Lior, suspended in the vastness of space, surrounded by an encroaching shadow that consumed the light, drawing him into a spiral of helplessness and agony. His cry echoed in her mind, a haunting sound that reverberated through her bones. The shadows whispered, slithering in the back of her consciousness, promising doom. They wanted him—no, they *needed* him—to fall.

With every dream, the feeling in her chest grew heavier, tighter. She had to do something. But what could she do? She was bound by an oath—an oath that demanded she protect the stars but never intervene in their struggles. Yet here she was, bound to the very star she was sworn to guard, feeling his suffering as if it were her own.

The dreams had started innocuously enough, quiet glimpses of Lior in his celestial realm, radiating warmth and life. But over the last few days, they had changed. The once beautiful glow that surrounded him had dimmed, and in its place, shadows crept in, twisting around his form. His cries were not only for help but for understanding. As if, in his weakened state, he was aware of something greater, something more dangerous that was pulling him into the darkness.

Isolde opened her eyes, standing once again at the tower's edge. The vast expanse of space stretched before her, but her gaze was fixed firmly on Lior's star. His light, though weak, still called to her, a flickering pulse against the black canvas of the universe. She could feel the tension in her chest, her heartbeat echoing with each faint pulse from Lior's dying glow.

She could not ignore the truth any longer—she was losing him. And in losing him, she could feel the universe itself beginning to unravel.

But was it even possible to save him? To save the very thing she was meant to guard?

The wind stirred around her, cold and distant, a reminder of the emptiness that had begun to settle into her bones. Her hand clenched around the railing, the cold stone biting into her skin, grounding her to the reality she was trying so hard to avoid. Her duty—her vow—had always been clear. She had never wavered before. But with Lior, everything felt different. It felt *wrong,* as though she were being drawn into something she could not control.

"Warden Isolde."

The voice behind her was low, calm, and carrying the weight of authority. Isolde's hand jerked away from the railing, her pulse quickening. She knew that voice. Alaric, the other warden, was always watching, always waiting. His presence was a constant in her life, a reminder of the rules that governed their existence. He would see the change in her, see how her attention lingered on Lior, how she no longer followed the orders of her oath as she once had.

Isolde turned slowly, her expression carefully neutral, but she could feel the heat rising in her cheeks. She had to hide the turmoil, the growing attachment to the star that threatened to unravel everything she had worked for. She had to keep her emotions in check, even as they threatened to drown her.

"What is it, Alaric?" she asked, her voice steady, betraying none of the fear that churned inside her.

Alaric stepped forward, his dark eyes scanning her face for any sign of weakness. He was tall, his frame imposing, and the way he carried himself spoke of years of discipline and adherence to their sacred duty. He had always been the perfect Warden, unwavering and steadfast. But now, there was something different in his gaze—a suspicion, perhaps, or perhaps the beginnings of something deeper.

"Isolde…" He paused, studying her with an intensity that sent a chill down her spine. "You've been spending too much time watching Lior. His light is dimming, yes, but it's not a cause for concern. You know this. The stars have their cycles. Some dim, some burn out. But they are not ours to save."

Her chest tightened at his words. He was right, of course. She knew that. *She* was the Warden—*she* was not meant to intervene. But how could she simply stand by and watch him fade? How could she ignore the pain that pulsed through her veins every time he faltered?

"I'm simply keeping watch," Isolde replied, keeping her voice as even as possible. "It's my duty."

"Then why do you look so… pained, Isolde?" Alaric's voice softened just slightly, though the edge of suspicion was still there. "You're not supposed to form bonds with them. You know that."

Isolde felt her heart lurch in her chest, her breath hitching in her throat. The guilt gnawed at her insides, but she couldn't deny the truth. She *had* formed a bond—whether it was fate or some kind of cosmic pull, she didn't know. But Lior had changed everything. And now, she had to make a decision.

"I'm doing my job," she said, though the words felt hollow in her mouth.

Alaric stepped closer, his eyes searching hers. He didn't believe her. And the longer this game went on, the more likely it was that others would notice as well. The other

Wardens were beginning to murmur, to notice her growing obsession. It was only a matter of time before her secret would be uncovered.

"Isolde," Alaric said softly, his tone turning grave. "You are the most dedicated of us all. But you cannot let your emotions guide you. You know what is at stake if you break your oath. If the celestial balance is disrupted—if you give in to your feelings—it will unravel everything."

The words hung between them, thick and suffocating. Her heart hammered in her chest, but she forced herself to stay calm. *Duty*, she reminded herself. *Duty comes first.*

But even as she thought it, she knew it wasn't enough. The pull she felt toward Lior had become too strong, too consuming. She wasn't sure what would happen if she let herself get any closer to him, if she allowed herself to feel the full extent of what she was afraid to acknowledge. She had already crossed a line. And now, it was too late to go back.

"I know," she said finally, her voice barely above a whisper. "I know what's at stake."

Alaric studied her for a moment longer before nodding, the suspicion in his eyes fading only slightly. "If you ever need help, Isolde," he said quietly, "you know where I stand."

Isolde nodded, but the words felt like a lifeline she couldn't quite grasp. She wanted to say more, to tell him the truth, but the reality of her situation was too heavy to share. If she revealed the full extent of her feelings, if she confessed her growing attachment to Lior, it would all come crashing down. She could already hear the whispers in the halls of the tower— the murmurs of distrust. If the other wardens found out, it would be the end of everything.

"Thank you, Alaric," she replied, her voice steady despite the chaos brewing inside her. "But I must stay focused. The stars need me."

Alaric gave her one last look, his eyes lingering with a mixture of concern and resignation before he turned and walked away, his footsteps echoing in the hollow stone halls.

Isolde stood there for a moment longer, her body frozen, as if the weight of the world had descended upon her shoulders. She turned back to the window, her eyes drifting once again to Lior. His light flickered again, weaker this time, and she could almost feel the darkness creeping closer, as if it were a living thing, intent on swallowing him whole.

She closed her eyes, trying to push away the pain that rose in her chest. But the truth was undeniable—she was in too deep. And as the shadows began to move around Lior, she realized that her decision had already been made. She could not protect him from afar anymore. No matter the cost, she would save him. Even if it meant breaking every rule she had ever sworn to uphold.

The balance of the universe was hanging by a thread. And only she could decide whether to cut it—or to save everything, even if it meant losing herself in the process.

The darkness was closing in, but she would not let him fall without a fight. Not without her.

Isolde's heart clenched with determination as she turned away from the window, her path set. She was no longer just the Silent Keeper. She was the one who would fight for the light—no matter the cost.

The weight of Isolde's decision pressed down on her, but there was no turning back now. The walls of the celestial tower seemed to close in around her, the vast expanse of the universe beyond only amplifying her isolation. The stars, the celestial beings she had sworn to protect, were no longer just distant lights. Lior had become something more to her—a presence that called to her heart in a way she could not ignore.

With every passing moment, the darkness surrounding him grew stronger. She could feel it in her bones, the way it clawed at the edges of her thoughts. The whispers from the shadows called to her, urging her to give in, to step away from her oath and surrender to the unknown. The pull was undeniable, like the gravitational force of a planet drawing in a falling comet.

But Isolde could not be swayed. She had spent her life guarding the stars, watching them from afar, never intervening. Yet, now she stood on the precipice of a decision that could destroy everything she had worked for—the universe's balance, her oath, and the very essence of who she was.

She turned away from the tower's window, her footsteps echoing in the empty halls as she made her way to the chambers that housed the ancient relics—the tools of the wardens. The glow from the celestial crystals cast long shadows along the stone walls, each one a silent reminder of the power they held, the responsibility they carried.

The moment her fingers brushed the cool stone of the relic chamber, the door slid open with a quiet hum. The relics, relics forged from the very core of the stars, glimmered softly under the dim light. She needed something, anything, that could help her. She could not face Lior with empty hands. She could not face the unraveling universe without a way to protect him.

Her gaze fell on the starlight blade—the weapon used only in the most dire of situations. It was forged from the essence of a fallen star, its edge as sharp as the pain in her heart. It was a relic that could sever the bonds of light and shadow, a weapon capable of cutting through the forces that threatened the stars. But could it save Lior? Could it stop the curse creeping into his light? She didn't know. But it was the only option she had.

She reached out, her fingers trembling slightly as they closed around the hilt. The blade pulsed with the energy of the cosmos, the power of ancient forces surging through her fingertips. She could feel the hum of the magic, the power that lay dormant in the weapon, waiting to be unleashed. Her breath caught in her throat as the weight of the decision settled upon her. Could she wield it—use it—against something as vast as the universe itself?

"I am the Keeper," she whispered to herself, her voice steady. "I guard, I protect. But I will not stand by while Lior fades."

The blade felt heavy in her hand, its power both comforting and terrifying. She wasn't sure how long she had stood there, her mind racing, the universe's quiet pulse resonating through her bones. But when she finally lifted the blade, a new sense of clarity washed over her.

She could save him. She had to. Even if it meant breaking everything she knew, even if it meant defying her oath and betraying the very laws she had sworn to uphold. She could no longer be the passive observer of his suffering. She would fight for him. She would fight for the stars.

Isolde left the chamber with the blade in hand, her heart beating in sync with the growing pull that led her toward Lior. She moved swiftly through the corridors, her steps growing more certain with each passing moment. She could feel the air around her grow heavier, as though the very fabric of the universe was aware of her decision, aware of the choice she was about to make.

The sky outside was darker than usual, the stars' light

dimming even further. The shadows in the sky were no longer just a distant threat—they were drawing closer, pulling at her with an insidious force. And she could feel Lior's presence like a heartbeat in the distance, fragile and fading, as though his essence was slipping through the cracks of existence. She had to reach him. She had to stop the darkness before it swallowed him whole.

When she reached the top of the tower, Isolde didn't hesitate. She didn't look back at the celestial relics she had left behind. She stood at the edge of the tower once more, her eyes locked onto Lior's star, which now shimmered weakly in the vastness of space. Her pulse quickened, and her breath caught in her chest. The connection between them had never been stronger, nor more painful. The star that had once burned so brightly was now a shadow of its former glory.

Without another word, she stepped toward the edge and, with a single, controlled breath, leaped into the void.

The sensation of falling through the fabric of the cosmos was unlike anything she had ever felt. The stars whizzed past her in streaks of light, their forms a blur as she fell deeper into the dark, swirling abyss of space. The coldness of the void wrapped around her like a shroud, but her body was warm with determination, the weight of the starlight blade heavy in her grasp.

In what seemed like an eternity, but also the briefest moment, she reached her destination. The swirling shadows around Lior's star seemed to pulse with an almost sentient hunger, reaching out toward her as though they recognized her presence. She reached out with one hand, her fingers brushing against the fading light of Lior's form.

Lior's voice echoed in her mind, faint but filled with an

undeniable strength. "You shouldn't have come, Isolde," he whispered, his light flickering violently. "It's too late."

"No," she breathed, her voice resolute. "It's never too late."

Her fingers clenched tighter around the hilt of the blade. The very air around them seemed to tremble, a flicker of magic coursing through the space between them. She could feel the weight of the curse, the darkness that sought to destroy him, but there was something else now. Her resolve. Her love. It was stronger than the void.

With a fierce cry, Isolde plunged the starlight blade into the heart of the darkness that surrounded Lior. The moment it made contact, a violent shockwave rippled through the cosmos, tearing through the shadows, sending them scattering into nothingness. The sky around them seemed to hold its breath, the stars themselves flickering in response. The blade burned with cosmic fire as the darkness writhed, as if it were being torn apart by the pure light of the weapon.

Lior's light pulsed one final time, brighter than it had ever been, and for a moment, Isolde felt his presence—strong, steady, and full of life. She felt the connection between them deepen, like the final piece of a puzzle falling into place. The shadow retreated, dissipating into the void as if it had never existed at all.

But just as quickly as the light flared, it dimmed again, and Lior's form flickered. A deep ache settled in Isolde's chest. She had saved him, for now, but she could feel his energy slipping away once more. The wound, the darkness, was still there. And they both knew that this fight was far from over.

She collapsed to her knees, the starlight blade still glowing in her hand, its power now fading as Lior's light did the same. The distance between them had not been closed, and though she had fought the darkness, there was a cost—one she wasn't sure she was ready to face.

"Isolde…" Lior whispered again, his voice barely audible but filled with a tenderness that pierced her heart. "You cannot save me. Not like this."

She shook her head, tears streaming down her face. "I will save you, Lior. I will fight for you. No matter what it takes."

But in the quiet, suspended moment between them, Isolde realized the truth. She wasn't just fighting for Lior. She was fighting for the universe. For everything she had once protected, for everything she had believed in.

And in this moment, suspended between light and shadow, she knew one thing with certainty: this was just the beginning.

The universe was watching. And it was shifting.

But Isolde, with the starlight blade in her hand and the love of a fading star in her heart, would not let the darkness win. Not without a fight.

And so, she steadied herself, ready for whatever came next. Ready to face the world—and the universe—with nothing but her love, her will, and the unwavering certainty that she would protect what was hers.

Three

Forbidden Meeting

The moonlight bathed the celestial tower in a soft glow, its pale light cascading over the high walls of stone like a whispered secret. Isolde stood at the edge of the tower once more, gazing out into the vastness of the night sky, her breath steady but her mind in turmoil. The stars above shimmered with an ancient light, distant and beautiful, but one star, in particular, had captured her every thought. Lior.

The celestial order was unyielding. She was bound by duty, sworn to keep her distance from the stars she protected, to never allow personal attachment to cloud her judgment. And yet, with each passing night, her heart twisted more painfully with every glance toward his fading light. She could feel his pull, like an invisible thread connecting her to his radiance, drawing her closer, threatening to unravel everything she had known.

It was a quiet, secret longing—a yearning she couldn't ignore, though she fought to do so. But the dreams, the whispers in her mind, had become impossible to dismiss. Lior's suffering, his pain, had bled into her own soul, leaving an ache that no amount of distance or discipline could ease. She could still hear his faint cry, echoing across the expanse of the universe, and it haunted her every waking moment.

She had to see him. She had to understand what was happening to him.

For weeks, she had resisted the temptation to break her oath, to approach him beyond the safety of the celestial tower. But tonight, something inside her snapped. She could no longer stand by, watching from afar, while Lior fought alone against the shadow that haunted him. It was against every law, every principle she had sworn to uphold, but the truth was undeniable: Isolde had fallen for the star she was meant to protect.

There was a place, hidden deep within the heart of the celestial realm, where the stars could be approached without fear of disturbing their natural order. It was an ancient, forbidden grove, where the stars, in their rare moments of vulnerability, were sometimes allowed to rest. The grove was surrounded by cosmic energy, a barrier of magic that kept out prying eyes. The wardens, however, had access to it, though it was never used. To enter the grove was to risk breaking the delicate fabric that held the universe together.

But tonight, there was no other choice. Isolde had to see Lior. She had to understand the shadow that was consuming him, and she had to find a way to save him, even if it meant defying everything she had ever been trained to believe.

With one final, steadying breath, she turned away from the tower's edge and began to move deeper into the stone halls, her footsteps silent as she made her way to the inner sanctum. The air around her seemed to hum with anticipation, the very atmosphere thick with the weight of her decision. She could already feel the presence of the ancient barrier that surrounded the grove, the faint pulse of cosmic energy vibrating beneath her skin.

As she entered the sanctum, the ancient gateway stood before her, a shimmering archway of starlight and magic, framed by ancient runes that pulsed with the energy of the cosmos. The air inside was thick with the hum of power, and Isolde felt her heart race as she stepped closer, her fingers brushing the cool stone of the archway.

With a whisper of incantation, the barrier shifted, the starlight parting like a veil, revealing the path beyond. The grove was unlike anything she had ever seen. It was a place where the very fabric of the universe seemed to bend, a realm where stars could rest, hidden away from the eyes of the wardens and the celestial order. The trees in the grove were unlike any Isolde had ever encountered. Their trunks were made of crystallized light, their leaves shimmering with the colors of distant galaxies. The air was thick with the scent of celestial blooms, flowers that bloomed only in the rarest of moments, their petals glowing with the light of the stars themselves.

And there, in the center of the grove, was Lior.

He was no longer a distant light in the sky. He stood before her, his form radiant but flickering, as though he were struggling to hold onto his true shape. His light was dimmer than it had been before, the once-vibrant glow now tarnished by the encroaching shadows. He was beautiful, beyond anything Isolde could have ever imagined, his form shimmering like a living constellation. His eyes, however, were the most striking—bright with the intensity of a thousand galaxies, yet filled with a quiet sadness that struck her heart.

Isolde's breath caught in her throat as she took a step closer, her heart racing. She had never seen a star like this before—never witnessed such a powerful being struggling against something so vast, so unknowable. He looked at her, and for the briefest moment, she thought she saw recognition in his gaze. As if he had been waiting for her, as if he had known she would come.

"You shouldn't be here," Lior's voice was a soft murmur, the sound of it echoing through the grove like a melody that resonated deep within her. The tone was gentle, but there was an underlying current of something darker—something painful. "The stars are not meant to be touched. The rules are clear, Isolde."

Isolde swallowed, her throat tight with the emotion she could no longer suppress. "I couldn't stay away," she whispered, her voice trembling with the weight of her confession. "I felt you, Lior. I felt your pain. I couldn't just stand by and watch you fade."

He sighed, his light dimming further for a moment, as if the burden of his suffering had become too great to bear. "You have no idea what you're asking, Isolde. To approach me, to interfere with the balance—it's a dangerous thing. You risk more than your life. You risk the very fabric of the universe."

Isolde's gaze softened as she took another step forward, her heart pounding in her chest. She could feel the warmth radiating from him, even as the shadows clawed at his form. It was a warmth that pulled her closer, a magnetic force that made it impossible to resist.

"I don't care about the rules anymore," she said quietly, her voice raw. "I care about you, Lior. You've been fighting this darkness alone, and I can't watch you suffer anymore. Please… let me help you."

For the first time, Lior's expression shifted, the weight of his sorrow giving way to something deeper, something more vulnerable. He stepped closer, his form flickering with the intensity of the stars, his energy swirling around them like a delicate storm. "The darkness is not just a shadow, Isolde. It is an ancient force—one that seeks to consume the stars, to tear apart everything that holds the balance of the universe in place. It's not something you can fight, not with your magic or with the strength of your heart. It is beyond anything you understand."

Isolde's heart ached with the truth in his words. She had always known that the stars held secrets, ancient powers beyond her comprehension. But hearing him speak of the force that haunted him—of the evil that sought to unravel the very fabric of existence—left her speechless. She had come to save him, to protect him, but now she realized the depth of the battle they faced.

"I don't care how impossible it is," she said, her voice resolute. "I will fight for you, Lior. I won't let you fall. Not alone."

Lior's gaze softened, a flicker of something like hope flashing in his eyes. For a moment, they stood there, connected by something unspoken—a bond that had grown between them despite the rules, despite the danger. She could feel the power between them, a force that was more than just cosmic magic. It was love. A love that could change the universe, a love that could undo the darkness if only they could find a way to fight it.

But that love, as powerful as it was, was a double-edged sword. The closer they drew to each other, the more fragile the balance became. The very universe they had sworn to protect was now at risk—because love, in their world, was forbidden. And every touch, every shared glance, only unraveled the delicate threads that held it all together.

"I cannot promise you that I can be saved," Lior said softly, his voice full of the pain of his centuries of existence. "But if you are willing to fight, to sacrifice everything for me… then we may stand a chance against the darkness."

Isolde's heart thudded in her chest as she reached out, her fingers brushing against his flickering form. It was as if the very light of the universe had become tangible in that moment, and her heart swelled with the depth of her feelings. The pull between them was undeniable, and the connection they shared felt more real than anything else she had ever known.

"I'll fight with you, Lior," she whispered, her voice steady, though her soul was shaken by the magnitude of what they were about to face. "Together, we'll stop this."

But as she said the words, a cold shadow passed through the grove, like a sudden chill on a summer night. The air shifted, and the ground trembled beneath their feet. The darkness—*the shadow*—that had been threatening to consume Lior stirred once more. The balance was tipping, and with it, the fragile threads of their love and the fate of the universe.

Isolde held onto him as the shadows grew more pronounced, a warning that their time together was running out. The battle ahead would demand everything—sacrifice, courage, and the strength of their bond. But no matter the cost, Isolde knew one thing: she would face the darkness with Lior, even if it meant tearing the universe apart to save him.

The universe itself seemed to hold its breath as the first true test of their love began.

The shadows thickened around them, swirling in the air like a living entity, a presence that seemed to consume everything it touched. Isolde's heartbeat quickened, her body instinctively tightening as the temperature around them dropped. It was as if the very air was being sucked out of the grove, drawn into the dark force that now loomed over them. The celestial barrier—the one that had once protected this sacred place— was weakening, and the dark force was seeping in.

Lior's form flickered violently, his once-golden light now a pale imitation of its former glory. His radiant glow dimmed even further, as if the darkness had found a way to eat away at him, piece by piece. Isolde's breath caught in her throat. This wasn't just a curse—it was an infestation, something ancient and relentless. It was as though the darkness itself had been lying in wait, biding its time, until it had found the perfect opportunity to strike.

"Isolde..." Lior's voice was barely a whisper, strained with the weight of his exhaustion. His light flickered again, casting eerie shadows across his ethereal form. "I've failed you. I've failed the stars..."

"No," Isolde said urgently, her voice steady despite the overwhelming surge of fear that threatened to drown her. "You haven't failed me. We're not done yet, Lior. You don't get to give up on me now."

Her hands trembled as she reached out to him, her fingers brushing his dimming form. The moment her skin made contact with his light, she felt an electric shock pulse through her, a wave of energy that seemed to travel all the way through her chest. It was as though a part of her soul had connected with his, a tether that linked them in ways she hadn't fully understood until now. His pain was her pain, his desperation was hers, and the weight of the universe's balance threatened to tear them both apart.

The shadows seemed to hiss in response to her touch, as though they were alive and aware, responding to her defiance. The grove itself began to distort—trees of light that had once stood proudly now twisted and shriveled, their brilliant glow fading into cold darkness. The stars above flickered, each one growing dimmer as if the darkness was spreading across the entire cosmos.

"No…" Lior whispered again, his voice full of regret. "The shadow is too strong, Isolde. It's beyond me now. I can feel it, clawing at me—*at us*. It's never been just about me. It's about everything. Everything we protect."

Her breath hitched, her fingers tightening around him. His words hit her like a physical blow—he was right. The shadow was not just attacking him; it was attacking everything the stars stood for. It was tearing at the very fabric of the universe itself. If they didn't act soon, the balance of everything—time, space, light, and darkness—would be lost.

But even in the face of this overwhelming reality, Isolde felt the spark of something deep inside her—a fire that she couldn't ignore. She had made the choice. She had come here for a reason. And though the cost seemed unimaginable, she couldn't let it end like this. She couldn't lose him. She couldn't let the universe burn.

Her voice broke through the weight of the moment, firm and resolute. "We can stop this. Together. You said it yourself—we are *connected*. That means we have a chance."

Lior's eyes, once full of warmth and distant light, now seemed clouded with sorrow, but a flicker of something else—something like hope—glimmered in them. "I never thought you would come," he murmured, his tone filled with awe and something deeper, a kind of sorrowful admiration. "I never thought anyone could care enough to fight this."

"I care," Isolde said fiercely. "I care enough to fight, enough to protect you. Enough to protect everything."

Her heart thundered in her chest, and she stepped closer to Lior, the shadows pressing in on her from all sides, threatening to pull her into the abyss. The weight of the universe seemed to collapse around them, the air thick with the pull of darkness. She could feel the pressure building, an unbearable force threatening to crush everything in its path.

Lior's light flickered again, more violently this time, and Isolde could feel the warmth of his form weakening, fading with each passing second. "The darkness is too much for us, Isolde," he whispered, his voice like a gentle sigh of surrender. "We cannot fight this. Not alone."

Isolde felt her heart wrench at the thought. Alone? They had never been alone. Not in the ways that mattered. She had always felt the connection between them, even if they hadn't fully understood it. Her presence, her strength—Lior had always been there, shining in the distance, calling to her. And now, in this moment of weakness, she would not abandon him.

"Not alone," she whispered. "But together. We fight together."

In that moment, a brilliant surge of energy erupted from her chest. It was a force she didn't understand but instinctively knew how to wield. Her magic, which had always been passive, dormant in the background of her duty, surged forward like an untamed river. The starlight blade, still sheathed at her side, hummed in resonance with her own energy. The magic of the stars was within her, and with it, the will to protect—*to love.*

The blade pulsed once, glowing with a light so bright it seemed to push the darkness back. Her fingers clenched around the hilt, and she raised the blade high, feeling its power merge with her own. A flash of light lit up the grove, pushing the shadows back with a force that seemed to split the sky itself. The light clashed with the dark like two opposing forces, locked in a battle of willpower and ancient magic.

But the darkness, insidious and patient, fought back with equal force. It twisted and writhed, growing stronger, more hungry as it pressed in on them. The universe itself groaned in response, the cosmic tension between light and dark shifting, bending, and threatening to snap.

Lior's voice broke through the chaos, trembling but strong. "Isolde, you *have* to stop this. The shadow will consume us both. You can't—"

"I *won't* let it," she interrupted, her voice shaking with determination, a fierce cry of defiance against the crushing weight of the universe's impending collapse. Her eyes locked onto his, feeling the bond between them stretch to its limits, the light of the stars burning brighter as the darkness faltered. "You are not alone, Lior. And I am not leaving you."

With the starlight blade in her hand, she thrust it into the heart of the dark force, letting its power channel through her. The shadows recoiled, shrieking in pain, but the darkness was far from vanquished. It twisted and churned around her, eager to snuff out her light, to destroy the very thing she had come to protect.

Lior's form flickered again, but this time, it was not only from the fading of his light. Something else was happening. A strange surge of energy pulsed through the space between them. Isolde could feel it—a resonance, a connection between their souls, a bond that neither time nor darkness could break. For a moment, the darkness hesitated, the pressure easing just enough to allow them a fleeting chance.

"Together," Isolde whispered, her eyes never leaving Lior. She could see the pain in his eyes, but she could also see the flicker of hope that had been reignited, no matter how small. His light brightened once more, though still faint, still flickering.

A sense of purpose surged through her, and with renewed strength, she tightened her grip on the starlight blade. She would not let the darkness win. She would not let Lior fade. Not now. Not ever.

In that moment, the shadows lunged at them once more, their tendrils stretching like hands of the dead, but they were met with a force stronger than either had anticipated—the combined power of a warden's devotion and a star's desperate fight for survival.

Isolde closed her eyes, feeling the energy between them pulse and surge like a tide of pure starlight. She and Lior, bound by something greater than the universe itself, now stood as one against the darkness. The struggle had only just begun.

But in this moment, surrounded by the very stars that had witnessed the birth of time itself, Isolde knew one thing for certain: she would not let the darkness consume him, no matter the cost.

Four

The Searing Darkness

The celestial realm had always been a place of quiet reverence, a vast sea of stars woven together by threads of light that pulsed with life and energy. But as Isolde stood at the top of the ancient tower, her eyes fixed on the swirling mass of darkness in the sky, she knew that everything had changed. The stars—those once steady beacons of hope and order—had begun to flicker, dimming as if some invisible force was draining their very essence.

The cool wind tugged at her cloak, but she barely noticed the chill. The pulse of the darkness grew stronger with each passing hour, threatening to collapse everything she had sworn to protect. The power that had once held the stars in place was crumbling, and with it, the delicate balance that held the universe together.

She clenched her fists at her sides, her fingers aching with the tension in her bones. She could feel the pull, the weight of responsibility pressing down on her chest. She had spent years as the Warden, guarding the stars from afar, but now, the threat was something far more personal. The darkness that had begun creeping across the heavens was no mere shadow—it was alive.

And it was drawing closer.

"Warden," a voice interrupted her thoughts. It was Alaric, his deep voice calm but tinged with concern. He stepped up beside her, his sharp eyes scanning the heavens. His expression was unreadable, but Isolde could feel the weight of his gaze on her.

"I know," she said softly, her voice barely above a whisper. "I can feel it, too. It's getting worse."

Alaric nodded, his jaw set in a hard line. "We've received word from the Star Elders," he continued, his voice low, careful. "It's Tharion. He's the one responsible."

Isolde's breath hitched at the name. Tharion. The fallen star. The one who had once been a protector of the celestial realms but had betrayed his brethren, drawn to a darkness so deep that even the stars themselves shied away from it. His fall had been a warning, a shadow over the entire universe. But now, the shadow was growing larger, threatening to engulf them all.

"Tharion?" Isolde repeated, her voice trembling with a mix of fear and disbelief. "He's alive?"

Alaric's eyes darkened, and he glanced at her, his expression grave. "He is. And his power is unlike anything we've encountered before. He's able to drain the very life force from the stars, to consume their energy until there's nothing left. It's as if he's feeding off them, growing stronger with each one he extinguishes."

Isolde's heart sank, a cold fear creeping through her veins. The stars were not just lights in the sky—they were the lifeblood of the universe, the very force that held everything together. To lose even one was a catastrophe, but to lose them all? It would mean the end of existence itself.

"How do we stop him?" Isolde asked, her voice tight with urgency.

"We need to confront him," Alaric replied, his eyes fixed on the flickering stars above. "We can't wait any longer. His power is growing, and if we don't act soon, he will consume the last of the stars. The balance will be lost forever."

Isolde nodded, her mind racing. But even as she considered their options, she couldn't shake the feeling of dread that had settled deep within her. She had never felt so small, so powerless in the face of such an overwhelming force. Tharion was no ordinary rogue celestial. His darkness was ancient, and its very presence twisted the fabric of the cosmos.

But there was something else, too—something that gnawed at her heart. Lior.

Since their forbidden meeting, since the moment she had first touched his light, their connection had only grown stronger. The bond between them had become more than just a tether—it was a force of its own, something that transcended the stars themselves. But it was also dangerous. She could feel the pull between them, a magnetic force that threatened to consume her, to break the vows she had sworn to keep.

Her love for Lior, though still unspoken, was undeniable. And yet, the universe she had spent her entire life protecting was slipping away, and the only way to stop it was to confront the very darkness that had begun to eat away at everything she held dear.

Isolde took a deep breath, steadying herself. The time had come to make a choice—to risk everything to save the stars and the one she loved, or to let it all unravel and watch as the universe she had sworn to protect burned.

"I'll do it," she said, her voice strong. "I'll confront Tharion."

Alaric looked at her, his brow furrowing with concern. "Isolde, you don't understand what you're saying. Tharion is more powerful than you can imagine. He's not just a fallen star. He's a force of nature. The darkness he controls… it's unlike anything we've ever faced. You'll be putting yourself in unimaginable danger."

Isolde met his gaze, her eyes fierce. "I know the risks. But I won't stand by while the stars—while Lior—are consumed by this. I have to stop him."

Alaric remained silent for a long moment, his face unreadable. Finally, he nodded, though there was a trace of reluctance in his eyes. "If you're determined, then I'll help you. But know this, Isolde—once we face Tharion, there's no turning back."

She nodded, her jaw set in determination. The gravity of their mission was clear, but her heart had already made its choice. She couldn't allow the darkness to swallow everything. She couldn't lose Lior—not when she had just found him.

Later that night, Isolde stood before the ancient portal that would take her to the heart of the universe, where Tharion's dark power was said to be at its strongest. The starlight blade was at her side, its edge glowing faintly in the dark, its power now intertwined with her own. Alaric stood beside her, his presence a steady force that calmed her nerves, but even he seemed uneasy.

"Are you ready?" he asked, his voice low but carrying the weight of his concern.

Isolde nodded, her heart racing. "I have no choice."

Alaric didn't reply. Instead, he stepped forward and raised

his hand to the portal's shimmering surface. The air around them hummed with energy as the gateway began to open, revealing a swirling vortex of light and shadow that stretched out before them. It was the very essence of the universe, a place where the stars themselves were born and died.

She stepped forward, her breath catching in her throat as the portal swallowed her whole.

The moment they passed through the portal, Isolde felt herself tumbling through the fabric of space. The stars twisted around her, their light bending in unnatural ways as the very fabric of reality seemed to warp. The air felt thick with a palpable darkness, a suffocating presence that seemed to claw at her very soul.

When the world finally stopped spinning, she found herself standing in the heart of the universe—a vast, barren expanse where the stars once shone bright but now lay in disarray. The very energy that had once radiated from them was now dampened, swallowed by the inescapable void that surrounded them.

In the center of the expanse stood Tharion.

He was no longer the brilliant star he once had been. His form was twisted, dark, and formless, his once-radiant light now a sickly shade of black that pulsed with a malevolent energy. His eyes, once filled with the wonder of the stars, were now pools of endless night, deep and full of the darkness he had embraced.

Tharion turned slowly, his gaze locking onto Isolde as she stood there, the starlight blade now in her hand, its glow the only thing keeping the shadows at bay.

"You've come," Tharion's voice was a low growl, reverberating through the space. "How foolish."

Isolde's pulse quickened, but she didn't flinch. She couldn't afford to. She had come too far to turn back now.

"I've come to stop you," she said, her voice steady despite the terror that gnawed at her insides. "The stars are not yours to consume. You are no longer a protector. You are a parasite."

Tharion laughed, a sound that echoed like the death knell of a dying star. "You think you can stop me? You think you can save them all?" His eyes flickered, the dark energy surrounding him intensifying. "You will never defeat me, Isolde. You are too weak. You don't understand the true nature of power."

Isolde raised the starlight blade high, its edge catching the faint light that still remained in the universe's center. "Maybe I don't," she said, her voice a whisper of defiance. "But I understand love. And that's enough to stop you."

The air crackled with energy as Tharion's form began to writhe and shift, the shadows growing thicker, swirling around him like a storm. "Love?" he spat. "Love has no place here, Warden. The universe doesn't care for your emotions. It only cares for power."

"Then we'll see what power really means," Isolde replied, her voice unwavering.

In a heartbeat, she lunged forward, the blade aimed directly at Tharion's heart. The darkness around him fought back with a ferocity that could only come from a being that had once been a celestial protector, now twisted by greed and hatred. The universe itself seemed to tremble, as if everything—light and dark, life and death—were balancing on the edge of a blade.

This was it. The final battle. And it would determine the fate of everything.

The blade sliced through the air with a deadly hum, its light dancing like the very stars it was meant to protect. But as it neared Tharion's dark form, the shadows lashed out like tendrils of pure malice, twisting around the blade, pulling it back with a force that shook Isolde to her core. She stumbled, her feet skidding across the fractured ground, but she didn't fall. The weight of the cosmic battle pressed on her, the very fabric of space twisting around them.

Tharion's laughter echoed through the void, deep and mocking. "You cannot defeat what has already consumed everything," he taunted, his voice low and full of malice. His eyes glowed with a dim, unnatural light, a reflection of his corrupted power. "Your love for the stars, for *him*, will not save you. It will only make you weaker, Isolde. I am beyond saving. Beyond redemption."

Isolde gritted her teeth, standing tall despite the crushing pressure of his darkness. She could feel Lior's light in the distance, flickering weakly, as if calling to her. The connection between them had never been more intense. She could almost hear his voice, a soft whisper in the back of her mind, urging her to keep going, to not let the darkness win.

Her grip tightened around the starlight blade, the glow of the weapon intensifying as she drew on the strength of her connection to Lior. The blade was no longer just a weapon—it was an extension of her will, of her love, of everything she had sworn to protect. She could feel its power surging, the cosmic energy flowing into her as the shadows pressed in.

She raised the blade again, and this time, the darkness hesitated.

"I *will* stop you, Tharion," Isolde said, her voice steady but filled with raw determination. "You may have turned your back on the stars, but I have not. I will *never* stop fighting for them."

The ground beneath her feet trembled as Tharion's dark energy surged once more. The air itself seemed to warp, pulling at the edges of reality, and for a moment, Isolde was swallowed by the void. Her body was weightless, suspended in an endless sea of blackness. The stars above her flickered, their light distant and unreachable.

This is it, she thought. *This is the moment where the balance is tipped. Where everything is either lost or saved.*

Her heartbeat echoed in her ears as she steadied herself, trying to focus through the darkness. She couldn't let herself falter. The stars needed her. Lior needed her.

A vision flashed before her eyes—Lior's flickering light, growing weaker, his form fading into the shadows. He was slipping away. If she didn't act now, everything would be lost.

With a roar, she surged forward, the blade cutting through the darkness once again. This time, there was no hesitation. The starlight blade shone brighter than ever, the glow pure and unwavering, as if it were the last beacon in a world on the brink of collapse.

Tharion snarled, his dark form shifting and swirling like smoke, trying to block her attack. But Isolde was faster, her body moving with a precision born from desperation and raw emotion. The blade cut through the air like a comet streaking across the sky, the light leaving a trail of brilliance in its wake.

The moment the blade made contact with the darkness, a deafening crack split the silence. The ground beneath them shattered, the very fabric of space bending and tearing as if it couldn't withstand the intensity of their clash. Isolde felt a surge of power—an overwhelming force—that seemed to pulse through the blade, through her, and into the very heart of the universe.

And then, for a brief moment, everything stopped.

The light from the blade flared so brightly that it swallowed the darkness, casting away the shadows that had consumed everything in its path. The stars around them seemed to breathe again, their light pulsing back to life, stronger than before. The oppressive weight that had pressed down on Isolde's chest lifted, and she felt a surge of hope—the stars were fighting back, the balance was being restored.

But as the light began to fade, the air around her grew heavy once more, and the darkness returned, swirling violently in the aftermath of their battle. Tharion's form reappeared, though it was no longer the twisted mass of shadows it had been. He was now a darkened silhouette, his once-brilliant light almost completely extinguished, leaving only a faint, sickly glow. The struggle had taken a toll on him, but he was still alive. Still dangerous.

"You think you've won?" Tharion's voice was strained, but there was a wicked, twisted edge to it. "You've only delayed the inevitable. The darkness *will* consume the stars. It always has, and it always will."

Isolde stood her ground, the starlight blade now glowing dimly, its power fading as the forces around them began to settle. She was exhausted, her body trembling from the strain of the battle, but her resolve remained unshaken. She had come too far to let Tharion's words defeat her.

"I won't let it," she said, her voice fierce. "I won't let you take them. The stars belong to no one but themselves. And I will protect them with everything I have."

Tharion's form flickered again, the shadows twisting around him like an angry storm, but he did not move. He seemed to pause, as if weighing something deep within himself. The tension in the air was palpable, thick with the weight of a thousand choices, a thousand consequences.

"You are a fool, Isolde," he said, his voice no longer laced with anger, but something else—something cold, calculating. "You think love will save you? That *his* light will save you? You are as naïve as all the others before you. The stars are not here to be protected. They are here to burn, to consume, to fade. And when they do, so will everything else."

Isolde's heart twisted at his words, but she refused to be shaken. Lior's light still pulsed in the distance, weak but present, and with it, a glimmer of hope. She couldn't let the darkness consume him. She couldn't let it consume the stars.

"I don't care what you say, Tharion," she said, her voice unwavering. "I've seen what light can do. I've seen it in Lior, in the stars that still burn. I will not let you destroy them."

The starlight blade pulsed in her hand, its glow intensifying, feeding off her strength and her conviction. She raised it once more, and this time, there was no hesitation. There was no fear. Only the certainty that she had to end this—that she had to stop the darkness from taking over everything.

Tharion's eyes glowed with a twisted kind of fury as he lashed out, the shadows gathering around him in a final, desperate attempt to consume her. The air around them grew thick, the very fabric of the universe shuddering under the weight of their battle. But Isolde was ready.

With a single, decisive strike, she brought the blade down again, the light of it cutting through the heart of the darkness, piercing the very core of Tharion's power. The force of the blow sent a shockwave rippling through the expanse, the darkness screaming as it was torn apart, shredded by the light of the stars themselves.

For a moment, everything was still. The shadows receded, the cosmic energy swirling around them like a storm being sucked back into the void. Isolde felt the pulse of the starlight blade in her hands, its glow slowly fading as the darkness was vanquished. Tharion's form, once twisted and malignant, now seemed to collapse into itself, his power dissipating like smoke in the wind.

And then, there was silence.

Isolde stood alone in the heart of the universe, the battle fought, the darkness banished—for now. The stars above her burned brightly once more, their light filling the expanse of space with hope, with life. The balance had been restored, but she knew that it was only a temporary reprieve. The darkness would return, and they would face it again, but for now, she had won.

But even as she felt the weight of the victory settle over her, there was something in her heart that still ached. Something that had not been fixed, not yet healed. The connection between her and Lior still pulsed, faint but persistent. She had saved the stars, but at what cost? And would their love be enough to hold back the darkness for good?

Her gaze turned to the flickering light in the distance. Lior was still out there, still waiting for her, but the battle had only just begun.

She took a deep breath, her body still trembling from the strain, but her resolve stronger than ever. She would fight for him. She would fight for the stars.

And she would not stop until the darkness was gone—for good.

Five

The Heart of the Tower

The towering walls of the celestial tower loomed like silent sentinels against the starry sky. Inside the ancient stone edifice, every hallway, every room, seemed to hum with the weight of history. The Tower had been built eons ago, its purpose a mystery to even the most learned wardens, and its secrets were whispered only in the deepest, most sacred chambers.

Isolde moved silently through the winding corridors, her boots barely making a sound on the cold, polished floors. The tower, despite its immensity, had always felt like a place of solitude, a space where the wardens could do their work without interference. But today, it felt more oppressive than ever. The walls seemed to close in around her, heavy with the gravity of her decision.

She had to find the Heart of the Tower.

For years, the Heart had been a legend—a mystical artifact

hidden in the deepest part of the Tower, said to hold the power to bind the stars and their guardians in ways unimaginable. The Heart was whispered to be the key to everything, the force that could unite light and dark, fire and water, life and death. But its true power was shrouded in mystery, known only to the highest elders, those who had sworn an oath to never speak of it.

But today, Isolde knew she had no other choice. The darkness that had begun to creep through the stars—its terrible, malignant force—was still growing stronger. Lior's light had flickered again the night before, more violently than ever before, and the pull between them had deepened, making her feel as though she were being torn apart from within. She had tried to resist it, tried to keep her emotions in check, but the truth was undeniable: Lior was not just a star. He was the last of an ancient line of celestial beings, protectors of the cosmos. He was the one who could hold the universe together, and the darkness was determined to break him.

Isolde couldn't stand idly by while the universe she had sworn to protect fell apart. She had to find a way to save him.

And so, she turned to the Heart, the one thing that might hold the answers. The Heart of the Tower had been sealed for centuries, hidden away in a chamber so deep that only the oldest wardens knew how to reach it. The elders had forbidden anyone from attempting to uncover it, fearing the consequences. But Isolde could feel the weight of her decision hanging over her, pulling her forward. She couldn't wait any longer. Lior's light was fading, and the stars—everything they had fought to protect—was on the verge of collapse.

As she descended the spiraling staircase into the lower levels of the Tower, a sense of unease settled into her chest. The air grew colder, the light dimmer, and the shadows seemed to grow longer with each step she took. It was as though the very walls of the Tower were watching her, silently judging her for what she was about to do. The elders had warned her about the Heart. They had told her it was a force of great power, a force that could not be controlled.

But none of that mattered now. Lior's suffering was too great, and the universe itself was on the brink of collapse. Isolde could feel the pressure building in her chest as she reached the base of the stairs and stood before the enormous door that led into the Heart's chamber. The door was covered in intricate runes, ancient symbols that pulsed with an energy she could feel in the pit of her stomach. These were not just markings—they were warnings.

Isolde raised her hand, fingers trembling slightly as she traced the symbols along the doorframe. The runes shifted under her touch, glowing faintly, as if acknowledging her presence. She had studied these runes before—though they were beyond the understanding of most wardens, she had spent years memorizing their meanings. They spoke of power, of life and death, of cosmic balance. But they also spoke of a price. A price that had never been paid, and one that Isolde had hoped to avoid.

With a final, steadying breath, she pressed her palm against the door. The runes flared to life, and the massive door groaned open with a low, reverberating sound. Inside, the room was bathed in a soft, golden light. At the center of the room stood a pedestal, and atop it lay the Heart—the source of the Tower's power, the key to everything.

The Heart was a swirling mass of light and energy, contained within a crystal sphere that seemed to float effortlessly above the pedestal. It pulsed with a rhythm that seemed to match the beat of Isolde's heart, a steady, almost hypnotic thrum. The air around it vibrated with power, the very fabric of the universe bending and warping as though it were attuned to the Heart's presence.

Isolde stepped forward, her heart racing as she approached the pedestal. She could feel the weight of its energy pressing down on her, like the gravity of a planet. The power within it was palpable, suffocating in its intensity. But there was something else, something more—the Heart was alive. It was not just a relic, an artifact of ancient power. It was a force, a living entity that held the key to the stars' existence.

As her fingers brushed the surface of the Heart, a shock of energy coursed through her body. She gasped, her body tensing, and for a moment, the room around her seemed to fade into darkness. A vision flooded her mind, a vision of a time long past.

She saw a great city of light, a celestial kingdom that stretched across the sky, its towers reaching toward the stars. She saw beings, like Lior, brilliant and radiant, standing side by side, guarding the cosmos with unwavering resolve. But then, there was darkness—a shadow that fell upon the city, a force of destruction that consumed everything it touched. The celestial guardians fought valiantly, but one by one, they were extinguished, their light fading into the void.

And then, she saw *him*—Tharion. A once-radiant star, now twisted and corrupted by the darkness, his power consuming the very essence of the stars. He stood amidst the ruins of the celestial kingdom, his eyes glowing with malevolent fire, and the stars around him dimmed. The vision faded, and Isolde was left with a sense of terrible loss, of something irreparably broken.

The Heart pulsed once more, and a voice—a voice as old as the universe itself—spoke in her mind.

The path you seek is fraught with peril, Warden. The Heart holds the key, but it also holds the price. To save him, you must forsake your oath. The balance you seek to protect may no longer be within your control. Are you prepared to sacrifice everything?

Isolde's breath caught in her throat. The weight of the question pressed on her like an anchor pulling her deeper into the abyss. The universe was crumbling, Lior was fading, and the darkness that had consumed Tharion now sought to devour everything. But the Heart was offering her something— a way to save him, to save the stars. But at what cost?

Her hand trembled as she lifted it away from the Heart, the pulsing energy still thrumming through her veins. She knew what the Heart was asking. It was asking for a sacrifice. A sacrifice of power, of duty. It was asking her to break her oath, to defy the very laws of the universe.

But she couldn't let Lior die. She couldn't let the universe fall to ruin because of a broken oath. The price of saving the stars—of saving everything—was too high, but she was willing to pay it.

"I'm ready," she whispered, her voice trembling but firm. "Tell me what I must do."

The Heart pulsed again, and the voice returned, this time with a note of sorrow. *The cost is great, Warden. But it is the only way. To save the star, to save him, you must bind yourself to him. His fate will become yours. You will no longer be a Warden, no longer the guardian of the stars. You will become one with them. And in doing so, you will cease to be human.*

Isolde's heart pounded in her chest, but her resolve only strengthened. To save Lior, to protect him from the darkness that threatened to consume him, she was willing to give up everything. Her duty, her humanity—everything. She had never imagined that this would be the cost, but the alternative was too dire. She could not allow the universe to fall apart, not when she could still fight.

"Do it," she said, her voice a whisper, her heart heavy with the weight of the choice. "I will do it."

The Heart shuddered, and a brilliant light engulfed her. The very fabric of the universe seemed to bend, to pulse, as the magic coursed through her. Isolde's body trembled as she felt the power of the stars flow into her, felt the weight of their energy filling her veins. But as the light faded, she knew something had changed. She was no longer just a Warden.

The transformation was complete.

She was now bound to the stars, bound to Lior, their fates intertwined. But as the power of the Heart flowed through her, she felt the universe itself shift around her. The stars were no longer distant lights. They were her essence, her breath, her heart. She was part of them, and they were part of her.

But with that connection came a great responsibility. She had broken her oath. She had defied the very laws of the universe. The balance had been disturbed, and now, there was no turning back. The weight of her decision pressed upon her like the weight of the heavens themselves. Isolde staggered slightly as the energy surged within her, a searing heat flooding her veins, mingling with a coldness that made her breath catch. She could feel the stars in her chest now, not just above her but inside her, their light flickering, burning with life, but also with an undeniable pull toward something darker, something that threatened to consume it all.

The chamber around her seemed to warp, the walls of the Tower bending and shimmering with the immense force she now carried within her. The very air crackled with magic, thick with the pulse of cosmic energy that had fused with her soul. The Heart of the Tower pulsed one last time, then fell still, its golden glow dimming to a faint, almost imperceptible hum.

Isolde's hand clutched her chest, feeling the heartbeats of the stars echoing through her. She was no longer the warden who stood apart from the light—she had become part of it, as it was now part of her. But with the weight of this transformation came an overwhelming sense of loss, an emptiness that gnawed at her insides.

"I've done it," she whispered to herself, though the words felt hollow in the vastness of the now-silent room. "I've done what had to be done."

But the more she thought about it, the more she realized what she had given up. Her humanity was slipping away. She had broken her oath, betrayed the very laws she had sworn to uphold. In fusing her life with the stars, she had abandoned her former life, leaving behind everything that had once defined her—her purpose, her identity, her place in the world.

Yet, in the very same breath, she could feel the energy of the universe swirling around her, a power so vast and beautiful it took her breath away. But it wasn't just beauty she felt—it was the burden. The responsibility. She could feel the stars, the pulse of their light and the tremor of their fragility. They were alive, but so too were they dying, fading into the shadows that slowly stretched toward them.

And there, amidst this celestial fusion of light and darkness, was Lior.

A sudden surge of longing erupted within her, sharp and desperate. His light flickered in the distance, still distant and weak, yet her soul cried out to him. They were bound now, more than ever. She could feel his pain, his suffering, as though it were her own. It was as if their fates had become one—their destinies tied to the fabric of the universe itself.

The sound of slow, deliberate footsteps broke through her thoughts. Isolde turned, her body tense, and saw Alaric standing at the doorway of the chamber, his expression unreadable, his eyes searching hers. The moment their gazes locked, a flash of realization passed between them.

"You've done it," Alaric said softly, the words heavy with both awe and sorrow. "You've bound yourself to him."

Isolde nodded slowly, unable to find the words to express the depths of what she had done. The power coursing through her was overwhelming, but it was nothing compared to the ache in her chest, the pull she now felt toward Lior. It was as if she could reach out and touch him, feel his light, even if they were worlds apart.

"I had no choice," she said, her voice tight, her throat constricted with emotion. "The darkness is consuming him. It's consuming everything. I had to act. I had to save him."

Alaric stepped into the room, his eyes never leaving hers, as though trying to gauge the full extent of the transformation she had undergone. He studied her, his expression softening as he finally spoke. "You've made a sacrifice, Isolde. But it's not just your oath you've broken. You've given up your humanity, your connection to the world you once knew. You are no longer just a Warden."

The words struck her like a blow, but they were true. She

could feel it, the loss of what had once been. There was no going back now. She was no longer a guardian of the stars—she had become a part of them. And with that change came an uncertainty she couldn't quite grasp. She was bound to the very fabric of the universe, but at what cost? What would become of her now?

"What does this mean for me?" she whispered, her voice barely audible. "What am I now?"

Alaric stepped closer, his gaze soft, yet filled with an unspoken sadness. "You are a part of the stars, Isolde. You are no longer bound by the rules of the Warden's oath. But you are also something more. You've taken on the weight of the universe itself."

A shudder ran through her as she absorbed his words. She had become the living embodiment of the stars, their light, their life force. But with that power came an immense responsibility—one that might be more than she could bear. Was she strong enough to carry it?

The silence between them stretched, heavy and suffocating. Then, Isolde's eyes narrowed, a sense of urgency rising within her. "Lior…" she whispered, almost pleading. "I have to go to him. He's still fading. I can feel him slipping away."

Alaric's gaze darkened, and his jaw clenched as he approached her, his hand resting gently on her arm. "Isolde, wait. You've just bound yourself to the stars. You don't yet understand what that means. If you go to him now, you risk—"

"I *can't* wait," she interrupted, her voice fierce, a storm of emotion building in her chest. "I can feel him, Alaric. His light is slipping away, and I can't let him die. I *can't* lose him."

For a moment, Alaric said nothing, his gaze searching hers, as if debating whether to stop her or to let her go. Then, with a heavy sigh, he nodded.

"Then go," he said quietly, his voice thick with both sorrow and understanding. "But know this, Isolde: You are not just a Warden anymore. You're something *other*. The power you've taken on will not only affect you—it will affect *him*, too. The cost of this bond… it's far greater than you realize."

Isolde looked at Alaric one last time, her heart pounding, but her resolve unshaken. She didn't have time for hesitation. The stars were dying. Lior was fading. The darkness was only growing stronger. She didn't have the luxury of waiting, not when the universe itself was on the brink of collapse.

She turned and walked toward the chamber's exit, her steps slow but determined, the weight of the Heart's power pulsing within her with every step. The connection to Lior, to the stars, was a tether she could not sever, no matter how much it threatened to unravel everything else.

As she stepped into the cool night air, the stars above seemed to pulse in rhythm with her heart, their light beckoning her forward. She felt Lior's presence now more than ever—a light flickering faintly in the distance, but still there. He was waiting for her.

With the power of the stars within her, she set her eyes on the horizon, the path before her uncertain, the stakes higher than they had ever been. The universe was teetering on the edge of destruction, and only one thing was certain: she would save Lior, even if it meant sacrificing everything else.

The stars were calling. And she would answer.

Six

The Price of Sacrifice

The silence of the celestial tower was stifling, the air thick with the weight of Isolde's thoughts. She stood before the vast, unbroken expanse of the sky, staring out at the stars, but her mind was far from their distant glow. In the time since she had bound herself to Lior's fate, the universe had been in a state of turmoil. The stars themselves trembled, their light flickering with a frequency that was unnatural, as if something—someone—was draining their very essence.

And then there was the darkness. It had grown bolder, more insistent. It had begun to consume the stars one by one. Tharion. The rogue celestial who had once stood among the brightest, now was a harbinger of destruction. His shadow stretched across the stars like a spreading plague, eating at the very heart of their existence, and with it, the universe itself seemed to fray at the edges.

Isolde clenched her fists at her sides, the pulse of the stars inside her growing stronger, but so too did the pressure. The stars were calling to her, but their voices were strained now, ragged with pain. She could feel the weight of their suffering as if it were her own, each flicker of their light a cry for help that sent shivers down her spine. They were dying, and she—bound as she was to Lior, to the stars—was helpless to stop it.

"Isolde," a voice called softly, pulling her from the depths of her thoughts. It was Lior's voice, but there was an undertone of something else in it—something urgent, something… scared.

She turned slowly, her gaze meeting his across the vast expanse of the room. He stood at the far end, his form glowing faintly, but even that glow seemed weaker than it had been. His radiance flickered, a delicate pulse that threatened to die out entirely with every passing second. It wasn't just the stars that were weakening. It was him.

"Lior…" Isolde whispered, her heart clenched in her chest as she took a step forward, instinctively reaching out to him. "What's happening to you?"

He shook his head, a pained smile curling at the edges of his lips. "It's not just me, Isolde. It's the stars. It's everything. The darkness, Tharion… He's attacking the very core of what we are. We can feel it. The stars can feel it. It's… consuming us."

Her breath hitched at the words. She had always known the risks of her connection to Lior, the cost of binding herself to him, to the stars. But now, the consequences of that bond were becoming clear. As Lior's light dimmed, so did the very fabric of the cosmos, as if his life was tethered to their existence. If he faded, so would everything else. The stars, the galaxies, the universe.

"No," she whispered, her voice breaking. "I can't lose you. I can't…"

Lior stepped forward, his eyes filled with an intensity that sent a chill through her. "You're not losing me, Isolde," he said, his voice low and steady. "But we don't have much time. The longer Tharion's darkness spreads, the more of the stars will die. I can feel it in every pulse of light, every flicker that grows weaker."

Isolde took a step toward him, her gaze locked onto his. There was no denying it anymore. The stars were dying. And if she didn't act soon, it would be too late.

"But what can we do?" she asked, her voice desperate. "We're too small, Lior. We're just… just a warden and a star. What can we possibly do against Tharion's power?"

Lior's gaze softened, his eyes filled with a mixture of sorrow and something else—something deeper. "You've already done so much, Isolde. But the truth is, there's only one way to stop him. Only one way to save the stars."

Isolde frowned, her brow furrowing. "What do you mean? What's the way?"

Lior's form flickered again, and he stepped closer, his presence almost overwhelming. The warmth of his light washed over her, but it felt fragile, fleeting. "The Heart of the Tower—the source of the power that binds the stars, the force that sustains the balance of the universe—it holds the answer. The only way to stop Tharion, to restore the balance, is to break the very laws of the stars."

Her heart skipped a beat. "What do you mean, break the laws? The laws of the stars are—"

"Unbreakable," Lior finished for her, his voice quiet but firm. "I know. But to save me, to save everything, you will have to give up what you've always been. You will have to bind yourself to me completely, to my fate. Our fates will become one. And once we are bound like that, there will be no turning back."

Isolde's mind raced, her breath catching in her throat. To bind herself to Lior—completely, irrevocably. It wasn't just a physical or emotional bond; it was something much deeper, something that would alter the very fabric of her existence. She was already one with the stars, but this was different. This would tie her fate to his. And if Lior died…

Her hands shook, and she clenched her fists tightly. "You're asking me to give up everything," she whispered. "Everything. My duty to the stars, my oath, my humanity… I'd become nothing but a part of you."

Lior nodded slowly, his gaze filled with the intensity of a thousand stars. "Yes. You would become a part of me, and I would become a part of you. But together, we would have the power to stop Tharion. We could heal the stars, stop the darkness from consuming everything. We would restore the balance."

A cold, sickening fear gripped her heart as she considered the gravity of his words. She would be giving up her very identity—her purpose, her connection to the universe. She would cease to be the Warden, the protector of the stars. She would be lost to everything she had ever known.

But the alternative was worse. Watching the stars burn, watching Lior fade into nothingness—her love for him, for the stars, could not allow that to happen.

"I don't want to lose you," she whispered, her voice raw with emotion. "I can't…"

Lior stepped closer, his hand reaching out to gently touch her face. His touch was warm, a stark contrast to the cold emptiness around them. "You won't lose me, Isolde. I promise.

But we can't stop Tharion without this. You have to decide. Can you give everything up for me? For us? For the stars?"

Her heart felt as though it were being torn in two. The love she felt for him, for the stars, for everything that had always been her purpose, collided violently with the sacrifice she would have to make to save it. She had never been one to follow her heart so blindly, to abandon the very laws that had defined her life. But this wasn't just about love—it was about survival.

She swallowed hard, feeling the weight of her decision press against her chest. "What happens if I do this?" she asked, her voice barely above a whisper. "What happens if we are bound together?"

Lior's eyes softened, his expression a mixture of sorrow and hope. "If you bind yourself to me, we will become one in every way. My light will be yours. But if I fall—if the darkness consumes me—then you, too, will fade with me. Our fates will be sealed."

The room seemed to darken as Isolde's mind raced, her thoughts swirling with the enormity of the decision. She could feel the weight of the universe pressing down on her shoulders, could feel the stars themselves holding their breath, waiting for her to decide. Her love for Lior was undeniable, but was it enough to sacrifice everything?

Could she really risk her own existence to save him? To save the stars?

"I love you," she said, her voice trembling, the words almost too heavy to say aloud. "But what if it's too much? What if we fail?"

Lior's face softened with the gentleness she had come to love. He reached out, cupping her cheek with a tenderness that made her heart ache. "We won't fail. Together, we can stop the darkness. But I need you, Isolde. I need you to fight for us. To fight for everything we've built. Everything we could be."

Her breath caught in her throat. The weight of his words, the finality of the choice before her, consumed her entire being. There was no easy way out. There was no way to preserve her life, her identity, and still save him.

With a final, steadying breath, she nodded. The decision was made.

"I'll do it," she said, her voice trembling but resolute. "I'll bind myself to you, Lior. We'll fight together."

Lior's face lit up with a radiant smile, and for a moment, the room seemed to glow with the intensity of his joy. "Thank you," he whispered, pulling her into his arms. "Thank you, Isolde."

She closed her eyes, letting the warmth of his light fill her, knowing that this would be the last time she would ever feel truly human. She was giving up her very existence to save him—to save everything.

As they stood there, bound together in both heart and soul, the stars above flickered one last time, their light strengthening with the power of their connection. But in the back of Isolde's mind, a new realization settled. This was just the beginning.

The darkness wasn't finished yet. And neither was she.

The moment Isolde and Lior stood together, bound in a way they had never been before, a deep stillness settled over the celestial tower. For a moment, it felt like time had frozen. The weight of her decision, of the sacrifice she had just made, bore down on her like a crushing force. She could feel Lior's heartbeat, the pulsing light of his essence mingling with her own. They were now one—no longer separated by the boundaries of their realms.

But that stillness was short-lived.

The stars above seemed to dim, their light flickering like the dying embers of a fire. The warmth between Isolde and Lior flickered, too—strong and steady for a moment, but fading ever so slightly with every heartbeat. The cost of their union was already becoming evident. She could feel it, the way the bond between them was tugging at the very essence of who she was. A part of her—no, *all of her*—was now tied to him. And if he fell, so would she. If he died, so would everything they had fought for.

Isolde closed her eyes for a moment, taking a deep breath to steady herself. The weight of what she had just agreed to felt overwhelming, like the entire universe was now watching them—waiting for their next move. Their fates were no longer just their own. They were intertwined with the future of the stars.

"I'm not ready for this," she whispered, her voice barely audible against the storm of emotions inside her.

Lior's hands trembled slightly as he held her, as if he too could feel the weight of their connection. "None of us are," he murmured, his breath warm against her ear. "But we'll face it together. You're not alone, Isolde. You'll never be alone."

The air around them grew colder, the once-stable warmth of their bond now edged with uncertainty. As the shadows of the universe seemed to stretch toward them, Lior pulled back slightly to look into her eyes, his gaze searching hers with an intensity that made her heart race. His light, once so brilliant, now seemed to flicker and falter, weakened by the immense power they had just shared.

"Tharion," Lior said, his voice grim, "he won't stop. The

darkness he wields… it's unlike anything we've faced before. Even with our bond, we're still vulnerable. He's still out there, and the stars… they're still dying."

Isolde felt her chest tighten at the mention of Tharion's name. The rogue star had once been one of their own, but his heart had become corrupted by power, consumed by a darkness so deep it threatened to consume everything. He was the force behind the spreading shadow, the one who sought to extinguish the stars one by one. But now that Isolde had bound herself to Lior, she realized that the stakes were higher than ever. If Tharion found them—found *her*—he would destroy them both.

"We have to stop him," Isolde said firmly, her hand gripping Lior's tighter. "We can't wait any longer. The universe is unraveling, and with every moment that passes, it gets worse."

Lior's gaze softened, but there was a shadow of fear in his eyes that had never been there before. "We'll have to confront him, but we can't do it like this. Not while I'm still weak. My light… it's fading. Every day that passes, it weakens more."

The realization settled in like a dark cloud—his light, the very thing that held the stars together, was dying. And with it, so was everything else. The universe was built upon the light of the stars, and without it, there would be nothing left. The balance would collapse.

"I won't let you fade," Isolde whispered fiercely, her heart breaking at the thought. "I will protect you, Lior. I've already given everything to save you. I will give more if I have to."

Lior shook his head gently, his expression filled with both sorrow and gratitude. "You don't have to. You've already done more than anyone could ever ask for. But this fight… it's more than just about me. It's about all of us. The universe itself is hanging in the balance."

Isolde took a deep breath, her heart steadying as she met his gaze. There was no turning back. She had already broken her oath, already bound herself to him. Now, she had to fight for everything they held dear—the stars, their love, and the future that was slipping away with every passing moment.

"We'll stop Tharion," she said, her voice filled with determination. "Together."

Lior's light flickered again, but this time, there was a sense of hope in his eyes, a glimmer of something that felt like victory, even in the face of the overwhelming darkness. "Together," he agreed.

But just as the words left his lips, the ground beneath them trembled. A low, guttural sound reverberated through the Tower, shaking the walls and sending a ripple of energy through the air. Isolde's heart skipped a beat, and she immediately felt the temperature in the room drop, the warmth of their connection faltering.

"The darkness…" Lior breathed, his face paling. "It's here."

Before Isolde could react, the room was plunged into an unnatural darkness. The stars outside—the ones she could still feel, the ones she had connected with—vanished from sight, as if swallowed by the very void they were fighting to keep at bay. The air turned thick, heavy with a presence that felt ancient and malevolent.

Lior stepped forward, his form flickering as if the energy binding him to the universe was beginning to fray. "We have no time," he whispered. "Tharion has found us."

And then, in the next breath, the darkness shifted, coalescing into something… something *alive*.

From the blackness, a figure emerged—tall, imposing, its

form cloaked in shadows so deep that it seemed to absorb the very light around it. His presence radiated power, an overwhelming force that made Isolde's heart freeze in her chest. Tharion had come.

"You think you can stop me?" Tharion's voice was a rasping whisper, yet it echoed through the room like thunder. "You think you can save this crumbling universe with your love? You are nothing but a fleeting moment, a flicker in the abyss. The stars are mine to consume. And so are you."

Isolde's breath caught in her throat as she stepped forward, standing beside Lior, her heart pounding. The bond between them flared, and she could feel the full weight of their connection, their power. But it was still not enough. Tharion was too strong, his darkness too vast.

"We won't let you destroy us," Isolde said, her voice steady, though her insides churned with fear. "We won't let you take the stars."

Tharion's form rippled, shifting in the shadows like smoke. "The stars belong to no one but me," he sneered. "And you, Warden, have already given up your place in the order. You are no longer part of the celestial realm. You are nothing more than a broken fragment."

Lior's light flickered again, and he stepped forward, his presence a steady glow against the oppressive darkness. "You won't take her. And you won't take the stars. I will fight you until the end."

Tharion's laugh was low and filled with a mocking bitterness. "You think you can stop me, Lior? You are but a shadow of what you once were. Your light is dying. You will be consumed. Just as everything else will be."

Isolde's heart pounded, and for a moment, she felt a terrible sense of dread. The very darkness that Tharion wielded was seeping into her own soul, filling the air with a suffocating weight. She could feel the pull of it, the way it sought to erode everything she had worked for, everything she had loved.

But in the next moment, a surge of power erupted from her, a force born from the stars themselves. The starlight blade at her side pulsed with energy, its glow cutting through the darkness like a beacon. She could feel the connection between her and Lior, the love and the power that had merged their fates.

"We will stop you, Tharion," Isolde said, her voice trembling with a fierce certainty. "No matter the cost."

Tharion's smile twisted into something cruel. "The cost will be your very soul, Warden. And when it's over, there will be nothing left but darkness."

The shadows around them began to thicken again, swirling like a storm ready to unleash its fury. The final battle was about to begin, and Isolde knew that this would be the moment that determined everything. If they failed, the universe would crumble, and everything they loved would be lost.

And yet, despite the overwhelming odds, despite the darkness that sought to consume them, Isolde stood tall, her heart set on one thing and one thing only: to protect Lior, to protect the stars, and to save the universe. She had already sacrificed everything—her duty, her oath, her humanity. Now, she would give everything to ensure their love, their bond, would not be extinguished.

Together, they would face the darkness. And together, they would fight for the light.

Seven

The Rift of Trust

T he celestial tower had never seemed so cold, the vast halls of stone echoing with every footstep Isolde took. The weight of the universe pressed down on her like an invisible hand, suffocating and relentless. Every room, every corridor seemed to close in around her, suffused with the same tension that had taken root in her heart. The stars, the ones she had sworn to protect, flickered weakly in the distance, their light now dimmed and unsteady, as if on the brink of extinguishing altogether. The darkness had begun to spread faster, its tendrils creeping into every corner of the heavens.

And amidst it all, Lior—her connection, her love—was fading. The pull between them had never been stronger, nor had the weight of their bond ever felt so suffocating. She could feel his presence within her, a steady pulse of light that matched the rhythm of her own heart, but it was weakening with every passing moment. His light, once bright and radiant, now flickered erratically, struggling to stay alight in the face of the overwhelming shadow that threatened to swallow everything.

As she moved through the tower's halls, Isolde's thoughts spiraled. The decision she had made—to bind herself to Lior, to sacrifice everything she had known—had come at a great cost. She could feel the consequences of her choice like a gnawing ache at the core of her being, a constant reminder that there was no going back. She was no longer a warden. She was something else—something bound to Lior's fate and the stars themselves. But as the darkness grew stronger, she couldn't help but question whether it was enough. Could love truly save the stars? Or had she simply doomed them all?

The door to their private chamber stood before her, a silent barrier between her thoughts and the reality she was desperately trying to avoid. She had told herself she would face the truth—whatever it was. She couldn't keep running from it. She had to know. With a trembling hand, she pushed open the door.

Inside, Lior sat at the edge of the great celestial window, staring out at the stars, his form flickering in the dim light, like a candle struggling to stay lit against the wind. The glow around him was faint, his once-dominant radiance now reduced to a soft, fragile pulse. His energy was slipping, and there was nothing she could do to stop it.

Isolde stepped forward, her heart aching as she looked at him. "Lior…" Her voice faltered, but she forced herself to speak, to bridge the distance between them. "What's happening? What's wrong?"

Lior turned slowly, his eyes meeting hers. There was a sadness there that she had never seen before, a depth of pain that went beyond anything she had imagined. His voice, when he spoke, was soft, almost broken. "I'm running out of time, Isolde."

She took a step closer, her heart sinking at his words. "What do you mean? You're the light, Lior. You're the heartbeat of the stars. You can't just fade away."

But even as she spoke the words, she knew they were empty. The stars were dying, and so was he.

Lior looked away, his gaze turning back to the vast expanse of space beyond the window. "I'm not just a star, Isolde," he said quietly, his voice thick with the weight of his confession. "I'm the last of a line, a line that has guarded the stars since the beginning of time. My existence is tied to the very balance of the universe. If I die, so do they—the stars, the celestial realms, everything. My death will mean the collapse of everything we've ever known."

Isolde felt as though the breath had been knocked from her lungs. "What?" she whispered, the weight of his words sinking deep into her chest. "No, that can't be right. You're the star that guides them, the one who keeps the light alive. How could you be the one to end it all?"

Lior's eyes flicked back to hers, a flicker of pain flashing across his features. "I never wanted this," he said softly. "I never wanted to be the cause of such destruction. But my death isn't just the end of me. It's the end of everything. Without me, the stars will collapse. The very fabric of the universe will unravel."

Isolde's mind raced, the information crashing over her like a tidal wave. Everything she had fought for, everything she had given up—her life, her oath, her duty to the stars—had been for nothing? How could that be? How could she have been so blind to the truth? She had thought that binding herself to him, to Lior, was the way to save everything, but now it seemed like it was the very thing that would destroy it.

"No…" Isolde breathed, her hand pressing against her chest as though she could push the fear and the disbelief away. "You can't be the cause of this. You can't."

Lior's form flickered again, his light dimming further as if the very act of speaking these words drained him more. "It's the way it's always been. The stars are my legacy. They are tied to me. My light keeps them burning, but when I die, they die with me. And the darkness will take over. It will be all-consuming. There won't be anything left."

Tears stung Isolde's eyes as the weight of his words settled on her, heavy and suffocating. She reached for him, her hand trembling as she placed it gently on his shoulder. "But we can stop it. We can still fight, we can still—"

Lior turned to face her then, his eyes sharp with a new intensity. "The darkness is already here, Isolde," he interrupted, his voice quiet but firm. "Tharion's influence is spreading. It's already been too long. I've felt his power growing, felt the stars flickering out one by one. And every time I try to fight it, my light fades a little more. I don't have much time left."

Isolde's heart shattered at his words, the finality in his voice cutting through her like a blade. She stepped back, feeling her legs tremble beneath her. The world—the stars, the universe— was unraveling, and she was helpless to stop it. Her love for Lior, her devotion to him, had brought them to this point, but now it felt like everything was falling apart. If Lior died, so would she. And if he lived, they might destroy everything in the process.

A deep, bitter laugh escaped her lips, the sound of it harsh and hollow in the silence that followed. "I never asked for this," she whispered, her voice trembling. "I never wanted to be tied to this fate. I just wanted to protect you… protect the stars…"

Lior's eyes softened, and he reached out to gently grasp her wrist, his touch warm against her chilled skin. "I know," he said quietly. "But sometimes, Isolde, we don't get to choose the path we're on. We are bound to the universe, just as the stars are bound to us. Our fates are entwined, and we cannot escape them. I never wanted you to have to make this sacrifice."

Isolde closed her eyes, fighting back the tears that threatened to spill over. The love between them had always been undeniable, but now it felt like a cruel joke. She was torn between her love for him and her duty to the stars—the very stars that were dying because of his existence. And she could feel it in her bones, the weight of her decision pressing down on her, suffocating her. She had given up everything for him, but what if it was all in vain? What if she couldn't save him? What if he was the one who doomed them all?

Lior's grip tightened slightly on her wrist, and she could feel the warmth of his energy flowing through her, a final flicker of light in the darkness. "Isolde," he whispered, his voice barely audible. "I need you to trust me. We don't have much time. But together, we might be able to stop this. I'm not asking you to choose between me and the stars. I'm asking you to choose us—to choose everything. Because if we don't, if we don't stop Tharion now, there won't be anything left to save."

Isolde stood there in silence, torn between the love that had bound her to him and the duty she had sworn to the stars. Her mind swirled with fear and doubt. Could she risk everything to save him? Could she defy the very essence of the universe to protect him from the fate that awaited them both?

With a trembling breath, she nodded slowly. "I will fight

with you," she said, her voice steady, though her heart was breaking. "I will fight for you, for us. But we have to find a way to stop Tharion. We can't let him win."

Lior's face softened, his light flickering briefly before flaring bright once more. "We'll fight together. And no matter what happens, we'll face it as one."

Isolde reached up and cupped his face, feeling the warmth of his light and the weight of his power pulsing beneath her fingers. In that moment, she knew what she had to do. She had already made the decision. She had already sacrificed everything for him. And now, she would fight to the end to save him—and the stars they both loved.

As she held him, the pull of their bond grew stronger. It was no longer just love that tied them together. It was fate. And as the darkness loomed ever closer, Isolde realized that they had no choice but to confront it. Together. For the stars. For the universe. And for their love.

The first step of their fight had begun, and it would take everything they had to win.

But Isolde was ready. She had no other choice.

The room around them pulsed with energy, and Isolde could feel the weight of the universe pressing down upon her. The power of the stars—their light—was now part of her, a constant hum beneath her skin, but with that connection came the knowledge that their fate, their lives, were bound to something far greater than their own desires. The universe had given them this path, and now it was demanding its price.

Lior's hands trembled in hers, and she could feel the fragility of his light, flickering like a candle caught in a strong wind. His power, once a radiant force, was slowly being drained, the darkness that Tharion controlled growing stronger by the second. It was like watching the heartbeat of the world slow, a pulse that was weakening, and Isolde couldn't shake the feeling that they were running out of time.

"I won't let you fade, Lior," she whispered, her voice thick with emotion. "I won't let the stars die."

Lior's gaze softened, his eyes filled with both gratitude and sorrow. "You've already done so much, Isolde. You've given up everything—your duty, your oath, your humanity—for me. I never wanted this burden to fall on you."

"Then don't let me carry it alone," she said, her voice steady despite the fear creeping through her veins. "I'll stand with you. I'll fight with you until the end."

A silence stretched between them, heavy with unspoken words. Lior's power was flickering again, and she could feel the pull of the darkness that was slowly consuming him. He wasn't just a star anymore; he was the very heartbeat of the celestial realms, and without him, everything would collapse. She had known this since the moment they had bound their fates together, but the truth of it—of how fragile everything was—hit her harder now than ever before.

Isolde stepped back, her gaze fixed on him, her mind racing. They couldn't wait any longer. The universe was crumbling around them, and Tharion's dark influence was spreading faster than they could anticipate. The Heart of the Tower, the artifact she had sought in hopes of finding a way to stop Tharion, had revealed something terrible—something that had left her breathless with its implications.

"To stop Tharion," she muttered under her breath, barely hearing her own words as they echoed in the quiet room, "we have to destroy him. But if we do, the stars will lose their light… and so will you."

Lior stepped toward her, his presence like a gentle but heavy weight at her back. "The stars have always been more than just light, Isolde. They are the foundation of everything—of the universe, of time, of life. Without them, everything would unravel. The only way to save the universe is for the darkness to be vanquished. But the cost… it's more than just mine to bear."

Her heart fluttered painfully in her chest. Was he suggesting that they had no choice but to destroy the very thing that they loved? Was she prepared to make such a sacrifice?

"I can't lose you," she whispered, the rawness in her voice trembling. "Not like this. Not when we've come so far. You… you're everything to me."

Lior's face softened, and for a moment, it was as if time itself stopped. The world outside—everything that was crumbling—faded away. It was just the two of them, standing together in the quiet, in the aftermath of the decision that had already been made.

"I'm not asking you to lose me, Isolde," he said gently, his hands lifting to cup her face. "I'm asking you to fight. To trust that we can still save the stars, even if it means confronting the darkness head-on. If we don't, if we hesitate, the balance will be lost."

Her chest tightened at the weight of his words. She had never felt more torn. The love she had for Lior—so deep, so pure—was a tether that connected her to him and, now, to the very fabric of the universe itself. But the stars—they were her life, her duty, her reason for being. She had dedicated herself to them. And now, her love for Lior was forcing her to choose between the two.

"We fight together," she finally said, her voice strong despite the storm that raged inside her. "We fight for the stars. For you. For everything."

The room seemed to grow still at her words, the air heavy with the promise of what was to come. And though she felt her heart tremble with fear and doubt, Isolde knew there was no turning back. There would be no more hesitation. She had made her choice.

Lior nodded, his eyes steady and filled with resolve. "Together, then. For the stars, for us."

Before she could respond, a low rumble shook the tower. The ground beneath their feet trembled as if the universe itself was warning them. Isolde's heart raced. They didn't have much time. The darkness was here.

Lior's form flickered again, this time with more intensity, his light pulsing weakly as though it were struggling against an unseen force. His hand tightened on hers. "The time has come, Isolde," he said, his voice strained, but there was a glimmer of hope in his eyes. "We must stop him. If we don't, everything we've fought for—everything we love—will be consumed."

Isolde took a deep breath and nodded. They had no choice now but to face Tharion—and the darkness he commanded—head-on. The power of the stars surged within her, their light a quiet pulse beneath her skin, and she could feel the connection between her and Lior, stronger than ever before. Their fates were now irrevocably bound, and there was no going back.

The door to the chamber creaked open, and Isolde's heart skipped as she saw Alaric standing in the doorway, his face pale, his eyes wide with urgency. "It's happening," he said, his voice tight. "Tharion is here. The darkness has breached the tower. We don't have much time."

Lior's eyes flickered, his form wavering as the weight of the situation pressed down on him. But his voice remained steady as he looked at Alaric. "Prepare the defenses. We need to confront him now."

Alaric hesitated for only a moment, his gaze flicking between Isolde and Lior. He understood now. The bond between them was undeniable. They were no longer just the warden and the star. They were something else—something much more powerful. And that power would be their only hope.

"Understood," Alaric replied, his voice filled with determination. "I'll do everything I can."

Isolde's breath hitched as she followed Alaric down the winding corridors, Lior's hand firmly in hers. The tension was palpable now, a suffocating pressure that built with every step they took. The tower itself seemed to groan under the weight of the darkness that was creeping into their very souls. She could feel it, that cold, gnawing fear that was creeping up her spine. Tharion was close.

They reached the central chamber, and Isolde's pulse quickened as she stepped inside. The stars outside had dimmed further, their light barely visible in the growing dark. And there, in the center of the room, stood Tharion.

He was no longer the brilliant, shining star he had once been. He had become a shadow of himself, twisted and corrupted by the very darkness he had once fought. His form shimmered, but it was no longer the radiant light she had once felt connected to. It was a hollow, fading glow, consumed by the blackness that now defined him.

"You've come, Warden," Tharion said, his voice a chilling whisper that sent shivers through her body. "I see you've made your choice. How quaint. But you cannot stop me. I will consume everything—*you* included."

The room seemed to close in around them, the air thick with the weight of his words. Isolde's grip on Lior's hand tightened as she felt his light flicker more violently, threatening to dim altogether. Tharion's darkness was overwhelming, but she wasn't going to let it win. Not this time.

"We will stop you, Tharion," Isolde said, her voice steady despite the terror that was trying to creep into her heart. "The stars will not be consumed by your shadow."

Tharion's dark laugh echoed through the chamber. "You think your love can save you? You think you can defeat me with your bond? I will tear you apart, Warden, just as I've torn apart everything else."

Isolde turned to Lior, their gazes meeting for one final moment. There was no time for doubt, no room for fear. They had made their choice. They were bound together, and now they would fight together.

"Together," Isolde whispered, more to herself than anyone else.

Lior nodded, his flickering light beginning to steady as the power between them surged. Their fates were entwined, and nothing—nothing—could tear them apart now.

The final battle had begun.

Eight

The Abyss Beckons

The universe had once been a place of order—a vast and intricate dance of light and darkness, where the stars were the keepers of balance. But now, the balance was slipping. It was more than just the darkening of the stars, more than the tremors that shook the heavens. It was as if the very fabric of existence was unraveling, fraying at the edges, the seams of reality strained and stretched by an ancient, creeping force. The darkness that had once merely whispered at the edges of the celestial realms was now a roar—an unrelenting wave that threatened to drown everything.

Isolde could feel it, the pressure building inside her chest, as if the weight of the collapsing universe were pressing down on her. She had never felt so small, so fragile. The bond she shared with Lior, the light that flowed between them, had been her strength, her anchor. But now, even that warmth felt like it was dimming, threatened by the cold shadow that loomed closer with every breath she took.

"Isolde," Lior's voice pulled her from the depths of her thoughts, his hand warm and steady in hers. She glanced up at him, his face pale, his radiant light flickering as it always did when Tharion's presence grew near. His form had been fading in and out since their bond had been sealed, his light becoming ever more fragile, as though the very act of binding himself to her had been a strain on his existence.

"I feel it too," Lior said quietly, his voice carrying a note of both despair and determination. "Tharion's power is reaching its apex. The darkness has already begun its assault. It will only grow stronger from here."

Isolde squeezed his hand, feeling the coldness creeping into her own soul. She had already sacrificed so much to save him—her humanity, her oath, her connection to the stars themselves—but was it enough? Could they, bound together in love and fate, truly stand against the coming storm?

The stars outside the Tower flickered again, a flash of light lost in the suffocating dark that had taken root in the heavens. Every pulse of the stars now felt like a dying breath.

"We must go," Isolde whispered, though her voice wavered with uncertainty. She was afraid—not of death, but of losing Lior, of losing everything they had fought for. They couldn't afford to hesitate. They had no other choice but to face the darkness.

Lior nodded, his expression tight, his eyes dark with the same fear. "The Heart of the Stars," he murmured. "We need to reach it before Tharion does. If we don't, there will be nothing left to save."

Together, they moved toward the archway that led into the infinite expanse of the cosmic realms. The walls of the Tower shimmered with the energy of the stars, but even they seemed dimmer now, the light they had once held fading under the weight of the darkness encroaching from every corner.

As they stepped through the archway, the world around them dissolved into the endless stretch of the stars. They were no longer in the Tower, no longer bound by the solid earth beneath their feet. The universe was a vast sea of light and void, a swirling, ever-changing expanse of shifting galaxies, nebulas, and distant stars. But even here, the darkness was present. It clung to the edges of the cosmos like a growing shadow, a slow, creeping tendril that seemed to stretch farther and farther with each passing moment.

"Stay close," Lior said, his voice soft but firm. "We can't afford to let the darkness get to us. The guardians of the cosmic realms won't wait for us forever."

Isolde nodded, her grip tightening on his hand. The bond between them had never been so palpable. She could feel the rhythm of his heartbeat, the pulse of his energy syncing with hers. But even that was starting to feel strained, like a rope pulled too taut. She could sense the fragility of the light inside him, the way it flickered beneath the weight of the darkness. Was this it? Was this the end of everything?

As they ventured deeper into the vastness, the stars themselves seemed to dim, their light flickering in response to the growing presence of the dark force. Isolde felt a chill creep into her bones, a shiver running down her spine as they moved through the void. She knew they were being watched. She could feel the eyes of ancient beings upon them—guardians of the cosmic realms, protectors of the stars, beings who had existed long before even the first star had ignited.

It wasn't long before they were approached by them.

From the depths of the stars, the guardians emerged—great, ethereal beings whose forms shimmered like the constellations themselves. They were creatures of light, their bodies translucent and glowing with the energy of the stars, their faces serene yet filled with a quiet, ancient sorrow. Their eyes—deep pools of starlight—studied Isolde and Lior, assessing them as they drew closer.

"You are the ones who have chosen to defy the darkness?" The voice of the first guardian rang in the air, both gentle and heavy, like the tolling of a distant bell. It was a voice that seemed to echo through the very fabric of space itself, vibrating with the wisdom of ages. "You are bound by fate, yet your love will be your undoing."

Isolde's heart raced as the weight of the guardian's words settled in her chest. "We are bound by the stars," she said, her voice unwavering despite the growing uncertainty in her heart. "We must stop Tharion. We cannot let the darkness consume everything."

The guardian's gaze softened, but there was no joy in their eyes—only the solemn recognition of what had been lost and what was yet to come. "Your love is pure, but it is not enough to stop the rift Tharion has created. The balance between light and dark, between the stars and the void, is delicate. You will need more than love to defeat him."

Isolde stepped forward, her heart heavy with the guardian's words. "What must we do?" she asked, her voice full of desperate urgency. "Tell us. We'll do anything."

The guardian's gaze flickered to Lior, then back to Isolde. "You have already given much, but there is one final step. To close the rift and stop Tharion, you must journey to the heart of the Abyss—the place where darkness was born. Only by confronting it at its source can you hope to stop it. But beware," the guardian's voice deepened, darkened. "The Abyss will test you. It will bring you face to face with your deepest fears. Your love will be tested, and the bond you share will either strengthen or shatter."

Isolde's breath caught in her throat. "The Abyss?" Her voice shook. She had heard whispers of it before—the birthplace of the darkness that had once corrupted Tharion, a place where the void itself was born, a place where the light of the stars could not reach.

Lior stepped forward, his hand still tight in Isolde's. "We will face it together," he said, his voice filled with a quiet strength. "We will face whatever comes."

The guardian regarded them for a moment, then nodded. "So be it. But know this: The Abyss does not forgive. It will take everything you are—your light, your fear, your very souls— and twist them to its will. Only those with true strength can survive it."

And then, with a wave of their hand, the guardians parted, revealing a swirling vortex of darkness at the center of the cosmic expanse. The Abyss.

Isolde's heart thudded painfully in her chest as she gazed into it, the sheer blackness of it consuming the light around them. It was a void that seemed to swallow everything—time, space, light, and thought. It was a place of pure fear, where the light of the stars could not penetrate, and even the bravest souls could be lost forever.

Lior squeezed her hand, his light flickering weakly but still there, a tether between them that could not be broken. "We have no choice. We must go."

Isolde nodded, her resolve hardening as she stepped forward, her feet moving through the swirling darkness toward the Abyss. The moment they crossed its threshold, the air seemed to thicken, as if the very atmosphere was trying to press them back. Every step felt heavier than the last, as if the darkness itself was trying to pull them under.

And then, they were inside.

The world around them shifted, the stars above them vanishing completely, leaving only the unrelenting void. The ground beneath their feet seemed to dissolve, replaced by an infinite, ever-shifting darkness that stretched into eternity. There was no sky, no light, only the oppressive weight of the void pressing down on them from all sides.

"Isolde…" Lior's voice was strained, his breath quickening as they continued forward. "I can feel it. The darkness is everywhere. It's trying to separate us."

Isolde squeezed his hand tighter, determined not to let the shadows take him, not to let the darkness separate them. "We're stronger than this," she said, though her voice wavered. "We've already come this far. We can't let fear take us now."

But the deeper they ventured into the Abyss, the more the shadows seemed to twist around them, pulling at their thoughts, at their emotions. The darkness whispered to them, soft and insidious, a voice that sounded like their own.

You are nothing. You are weak. You are not meant to exist. You are just a fleeting moment in the vast emptiness of the universe.

The words echoed in Isolde's mind, and she could feel herself falter, her steps slowing. The shadows pressed against her, cold and suffocating, but she forced herself to keep moving.

"Isolde," Lior whispered again, his voice thick with pain. "It's getting harder to breathe. I can't keep going."

She turned to him, her heart aching at the sight of his

flickering light, now barely visible. She could feel the bond between them—faint, weakening—and a cold terror spread through her. *If he fades completely...* she thought, and the sheer thought of it threatened to shatter her resolve.

"We can't stop now, Lior," she said fiercely. "We have to face the darkness. Together. Please."

With a final breath, she pulled him forward, stepping deeper into the void, her love and her fear driving her forward. They had come too far, sacrificed too much. They couldn't turn back. Not now.

The Abyss was waiting. And it would test them in ways they couldn't yet understand. But they had no choice but to face it. Together.

As they ventured deeper into the Abyss, the air grew colder, each breath coming slower, heavier, as though the very atmosphere was fighting against them. The light from Lior's form flickered weakly, struggling to stay alight in the oppressive blackness, while the bond between them seemed to stretch thinner with every step. Isolde could feel it—her very soul reaching out for him, tethered by an invisible thread, but even that thread was growing taut, trembling in the face of the darkness around them.

The shadows seemed alive here, undulating like a living entity, creeping into every crack, every crevice. They pressed in on all sides, suffocating them, whispering words that were not their own, words meant to break their spirits.

You are weak, Isolde. You are nothing but a fleeting moment. You think you can save him? You think you can defy fate?

Her heart pounded against her chest, the whispers grating against her mind like nails on stone. She could feel herself unraveling, bit by bit, the darkness seeping into her thoughts, clouding her vision.

"Lior…" She whispered his name, the tremor in her voice betraying her fear. She turned to face him, reaching out as if to anchor herself to his light. He stood beside her, still flickering, but the faint glow of his presence comforted her in a way nothing else could.

But even his warmth seemed dimmer now, fragile against the encroaching void.

"I'm here," he whispered, his voice hoarse, his breath shallow. "Isolde, don't listen to it. It's trying to tear us apart, to make us doubt. But we *can* face this. We can *do* this."

Isolde nodded, though the words didn't feel real to her. They were fighting something far older and deeper than anything they had ever faced. This wasn't just darkness—it was a force of pure destruction, a primal force that sought to undo everything they had built, to unravel not just their bond but everything the universe had ever known.

But despite the gnawing fear in her chest, despite the feeling that they were on the edge of something irreparably broken, Isolde refused to give in. She had chosen this path. She had chosen to fight for him, for the stars, for the balance that had always held the cosmos together.

"We will face this," she said with more conviction than she felt, tightening her grip on Lior's hand, feeling his warmth still there, despite the shadows pressing against them. "I won't let this destroy us. I won't let it take you, Lior."

The darkness rippled as if reacting to her words, swirling around them, growing thicker, darker. The shadows seemed to pulse with a terrible, unnatural energy, and the air became unbearably still.

In that silence, a low, guttural sound broke through—something between a growl and a whisper, an ominous presence that seemed to coil around them.

You cannot defy me.

The voice was a harsh, rasping sound that reverberated through their bones, a cold and malevolent echo that came from all directions. Isolde froze, her heart lurching in her chest. That voice—it was Tharion. It was the very essence of the darkness they had been fighting.

Tharion, the fallen star. The one who had once been a protector of the stars but now existed only to corrupt, to destroy. His presence surrounded them, suffocating them. Isolde could feel him in the very air, in the darkness that pressed in on them from all sides.

You cannot defeat me, Tharion's voice echoed again, now deep, vibrating with the power of centuries. *I was born from the void. I am the void. The darkness that will devour everything you love, everything you are.*

Lior's light flickered again, barely visible against the crushing shadow, and Isolde could feel the strain of the bond between them. His life force—his very essence—was weakening, just as the stars around them were fading. She could sense it—their fates were tied together, and if Lior fell, so would she.

"No," she said, her voice shaking but determined. "You will not win. We will stop you."

Tharion's laughter filled the space, hollow and twisted, as if the very sound of it was a rip in reality itself. *You cannot stop me, Isolde. You are just one mortal, bound to a dying star. Your love will not save you, for I have already devoured it. I have consumed everything.*

Isolde shook her head fiercely, trying to push the weight

of Tharion's words away, trying to focus on Lior. He was flickering, the light in him dimming once more, but there was something in his eyes—something that she had seen in the stars themselves. A quiet defiance. He wasn't gone yet. Not while they still had a chance.

"Lior, don't listen to him!" Isolde cried out, her voice full of desperation. "We are not alone. We *have* each other."

Lior's form shimmered in and out of focus, but there was a spark in his eyes—something that told her he was still fighting, still there.

"I am not alone," he said, his voice a faint echo but still strong. "Neither are you, Isolde. We are bound together, and we will not be broken."

The air around them seemed to shudder at his words, and for a brief moment, the darkness faltered. Isolde felt a surge of power, a pulse of light that flowed through her and into Lior. Their bond flared with intensity, and she realized that they were not powerless. They were more than just two beings— they were *one*, their fates entwined in a way that no darkness could sever.

But even as that realization hit her, the shadows closed in again, heavier, thicker. The Abyss itself seemed to grow larger, stretching further than she could see, consuming everything in its path. The rift between light and dark was widening, and the weight of it pressed against them, suffocating them in its darkness.

This is the end, Tharion's voice whispered, soft and deadly. *This is where it all crumbles. Your love, your connection—it cannot save you.*

The shadows surged forward, and Isolde's pulse quickened. She could feel Lior's light growing dimmer by the second.

If they didn't act soon, he would fade into the void, and everything they had fought for would be lost.

"Lior…" she whispered, her voice filled with a raw, desperate edge. "I will not lose you. I can't."

She reached for him, her hand trembling as she grasped his, feeling the faint pulse of his light beneath her touch. It was there, weak, fading, but still present. The bond between them had never been stronger.

In that moment, something shifted. The darkness around them seemed to recoil, as if it recognized the strength of their bond. The shadows were no longer just a threat. They were *afraid*.

Isolde's heart beat faster as she understood. The darkness had underestimated them. The power of their connection was more than just a fragile light. It was the essence of the stars themselves, a force that Tharion could not comprehend.

With a final, desperate surge of strength, she lifted her hand to the dark expanse before them. The starlight blade, now glowing brighter than ever, pulsed in her grip, its edge burning with the combined power of their love and the stars' ancient energy. She could feel Lior's light with hers, together, stronger than ever before.

"Together," she whispered, more to herself than to him.

Lior's form flickered one last time, his light blindingly bright. "Together," he echoed, his voice full of strength, determination, and love.

The starlight blade thrummed with power as Isolde swung it forward, a flash of light cutting through the darkness with a force that sent ripples through the fabric of the universe itself. The shadows shrieked as they were torn apart, and for a moment, the Abyss itself seemed to tremble.

But the fight was far from over. The darkness recoiled, but it wasn't done. Tharion's presence lingered, like a storm ready to surge again. And Isolde knew that this was only the beginning.

The final battle between light and dark had begun, and there would be no turning back.

Their fates were sealed, but together, they would fight. For the stars. For each other. For everything that had ever been.

And in that moment, Isolde realized that love—true love—was the only weapon they had left. And it was a weapon Tharion could never understand.

The battle for the universe, for life itself, was about to reach its breaking point.

And only they had the power to stop it.

Nine

The Shattered Realm

The dark expanse of the Abyss stretched out before them, an endless, consuming void that seemed to stretch into eternity. Isolde could feel the very air thickening around them, the oppressive weight of the darkness pressing in from every direction, suffocating and relentless. The stars—once brilliant and full of life—had all but vanished, consumed by the shadow that now blanketed the universe. The silence was deafening, a hollow void where even the faintest hum of celestial energy had disappeared.

Lior's hand gripped hers tightly, his presence at her side the only source of warmth in the cold expanse. His light had dimmed again, flickering in and out like a dying star, and with each passing moment, Isolde felt the bond between them strain. The darkness was relentless, and it was taking everything from them.

"We're close," Lior whispered, his voice barely audible as it was swallowed by the vast emptiness. "I can feel him, Isolde. Tharion is here."

Isolde nodded, her heart pounding in her chest. She could feel it too—the overwhelming presence of the fallen star, the force that had once protected the universe but now sought only to destroy it. Tharion's power was unlike anything they had ever faced, and his darkness seemed to echo throughout the very fabric of the universe. It was as if the very cosmos itself trembled under his weight.

Lior's light flickered again, and Isolde tightened her grip on his hand, feeling the frailty of his power. His energy was slowly fading, drained by the vastness of the Abyss, by Tharion's influence. The bond they shared was their only strength now, and yet, even that seemed to be slipping through their fingers.

"I won't let him win," Isolde murmured, her voice firm despite the fear gnawing at her. "We've come this far, Lior. We can't let him take everything."

But even as she spoke the words, doubt gnawed at her. Was it enough? Could love truly conquer this? Could they— *she*—really face the force that Tharion had become?

The answer came quickly, violently.

A sudden crackle of energy broke the stillness, sharp and unnerving, as if the very fabric of reality was tearing apart. The air grew thick with the weight of it, the oppressive darkness pressing in from all sides. And then, as if summoned by the very fabric of the Abyss itself, Tharion appeared.

His form emerged from the shadows, tall and imposing, his silhouette bathed in an aura of sickly darkness. The very air around him seemed to warp, the stars themselves trembling as he moved. His once-radiant form had been consumed by the shadows, and in its place stood a creature of pure malice, his eyes glowing with an unnatural fire. His power radiated from him like an overwhelming storm, and Isolde felt its weight crushing her chest.

"You've come to face me, then," Tharion said, his voice smooth, almost mocking, yet laced with the pain of years of suffering. His voice had a strange, familiar timbre to it, one that seemed to echo through the very core of Isolde's being. It was the voice of someone she had once known—a protector, a guardian—before the darkness had consumed him. "How fitting. But you should have known, Warden, that the stars were never meant to be protected. They were always meant to fall."

Lior stepped forward, his body flickering with weak light, but his voice was strong. "You've let your bitterness and jealousy destroy you, Tharion. The stars are not your property. They were never meant to be controlled."

Tharion's laugh echoed through the vast emptiness, dark and twisted. "Jealousy?" he scoffed, the word falling from his lips like a bitter curse. "No. It was love. A love that turned into something darker. I loved the stars more than anything, more than myself. And when I saw their fragility, when I saw them flicker and fade in the face of this universe's inevitability, I knew I had to save them. I had to *control* them. They are mine to command. And now, I'll make you an offer, Isolde. One that you can't refuse."

Isolde's heart raced, her pulse quickening with the rising tension in the air. "What offer?" she demanded, her voice sharp with defiance, though doubt lingered in the corners of her mind. What could Tharion possibly offer her that would sway her from the path she had chosen?

Tharion smiled, a cruel twist of his lips that sent a shiver down her spine. "I will make you an immortal, Warden. You will no longer be bound by your fleeting human life. You will have the power to control the stars, to command the very forces of the universe. Join me, and we will reshape the cosmos together. The stars will burn brighter than they ever have, and the universe will be ours to command."

Isolde's breath caught in her throat. Immortality. Power. The ability to control the stars themselves—everything she had ever wanted, everything she had devoted her life to. The temptation was real. She had always longed to protect the stars, to keep them from fading, from succumbing to the darkness. But could she truly accept Tharion's offer? Could she join him, knowing what he had become?

"And what of Lior?" Isolde asked, her voice shaking with the weight of the question. "What of the stars? You're willing to tear apart everything just to control it?"

Tharion's expression darkened, his eyes flashing with something ancient and bitter. "Lior is nothing. He is a dying star, a relic of a past era. He will burn out, and his light will fade, just like the others. If you choose him, if you choose to protect the stars, you will doom yourself. You will never achieve the power you deserve. But if you join me... if you embrace the darkness... you will be eternal. You will shape the future. The stars will burn as you command them."

Isolde's mind reeled as the weight of his words settled over her. The darkness was tempting, seductive in its promise of power, of control. For a brief, terrifying moment, she imagined what it would be like—no longer a mere warden, no longer a fleeting mortal bound by time. She could feel the pull of Tharion's offer in the pit of her stomach, a siren call that whispered of immortality, of a place where she could ensure the stars never dimmed, never faltered.

But then, she looked at Lior. His flickering light, the fragile pulse of his existence, was the anchor she needed to remember what truly mattered. She could see the fear in his eyes, the same fear that clung to her heart, and it broke her.

"No," she said, her voice trembling with the force of her decision. "I will not join you. I will never be part of your darkness."

Tharion's eyes darkened, his smile fading into a scowl. "You fool," he hissed, his voice filled with venom. "You are choosing a dying star over eternal life. You are choosing *him* over the universe itself. You are a fool to refuse my gift."

Lior stepped forward, his form flickering dangerously, but his voice was steady. "And you are a shadow of what you once were, Tharion. Your love for the stars was true, once. But you've let your jealousy and anger consume you. You've lost your way."

Tharion's form rippled, the darkness swirling around him like an engulfing storm. "You think I've lost my way?" he snarled. "I will show you just how much you've underestimated me."

Before either of them could react, Tharion's darkness surged forward, a wave of energy so intense that it shattered the very air around them. The stars above them screamed, their light flaring and dimming as the darkness consumed the heavens. Isolde felt the surge of power ripple through her, a force so strong it threatened to tear them apart. The bond between her and Lior pulsed, desperately trying to hold them together, but the pull of the void was suffocating.

"Isolde!" Lior cried, his voice desperate. "We have to fight back! We can't let him win!"

The room around them distorted, the walls warping and crumbling as the very universe seemed to tremble beneath the weight of Tharion's assault. The stars above, once bright and burning, were now fading, their light snuffed out like candles in a storm. The very fabric of reality seemed to tear at the edges as Tharion's power reached its peak, threatening to swallow everything.

But Isolde's heart, heavy with the weight of their choice, knew what had to be done. The darkness could not be allowed to consume the stars. She would not let it. With a forceful surge, she reached out to Lior, feeling the bond between them flare with renewed strength.

"We have to unite our light, Lior," she said, her voice steady now, her heart filled with a new resolve. "We are stronger than his darkness. We *are* the stars."

Lior's flickering form steadied as he locked eyes with hers, his light flaring brighter. "Together," he said, his voice full of purpose, full of the strength they had always shared.

The darkness recoiled, sensing their unity, sensing their strength. Tharion's eyes narrowed in fury. "You think you can stop me? You think your pathetic light can outshine me?"

But Isolde and Lior stood together, their light merging into one powerful pulse that radiated through the void. It was a force of pure brilliance, a beacon that cut through the darkness with a blinding flash. The light surged forward, breaking through the swirling shadows, tearing them apart piece by piece.

Tharion screamed, a sound that reverberated through the very core of the universe, his form writhing in agony as the light consumed him. But even as the light surged, Isolde could feel the strain—the darkness was not vanquished, not yet. The battle was far from over.

Lior's light flickered again, weaker now, but he stood firm, his hand tight in Isolde's. "We have to finish this," he said, his voice strained, but filled with unwavering determination.

Isolde nodded, her resolve hardening. Together, they would face this darkness. Together, they would protect the stars. And whatever the cost, they would never surrender.

The final battle had begun.

The overwhelming power of their light surged, engulfing the darkness, yet even as it tore through the blackened void, Isolde could feel the resistance from Tharion. The force of his malevolent power wasn't something that could be simply vanquished by a single wave of light. He was the manifestation of everything the universe had feared: jealousy, rage, and corruption that had festered for centuries.

But Isolde and Lior were united in their defiance. She could feel their hearts beating in time with the stars, their bond burning brighter as the light they commanded became more concentrated, more focused.

"Push harder," Lior urged, his voice strained with the effort, his form flickering dangerously. "We can't let him take us."

Isolde gritted her teeth, her eyes locked onto the figure of Tharion, who seemed to grow larger with every breath. The darkness around him writhed like a living thing, resisting their every effort, trying to crush the light, but they could not let it win. Not now. Not when everything was on the line.

The force of their combined light pulsed like a heartbeat, a flare of energy that threatened to tear apart the very fabric of space around them. The shadows recoiled, screeching as the light ate away at them, but the darkness was not easily defeated.

Tharion's form distorted, twisting and contorting as the light surged toward him, but his voice remained powerful, mocking, cruel.

"You think you can undo what has been done?" Tharion's voice slithered through the air, a twisted whisper that made Isolde's blood run cold. "You think this—*this*—is enough to stop me?"

The shadows surrounding him coiled tighter, and Isolde's heart faltered. She could feel Lior's light flickering weaker with every moment, his presence waning, and she knew that time was running out. She couldn't hold on forever. The Abyss was a chasm that would consume them both if they did not finish this. Tharion was trying to break them, just as he had broken himself.

"I loved the stars," Tharion said, his voice softening, a trace of the man he had once been breaking through. "I loved them more than anything. And yet, the universe turned its back on me. I gave everything. *Everything*."

Isolde's breath caught in her throat as she heard the pain in his voice. For a moment, she saw him—not as the dark, corrupted being before her, but as the protector he had once been. The star that had given everything for the sake of balance.

But then the darkness swirled around him once more, and she saw what he had become—the monster, the tyrant who sought to control the stars, who had torn apart the universe in his desperate attempt to remake it in his image.

Lior's light flickered again, almost going out completely. Isolde squeezed his hand tighter, desperation lacing her voice. "We cannot let him win. You *are* the stars, Lior. You *are* the light."

Tharion's dark laughter echoed again, and the world around

them seemed to warp, twisting as if the very essence of reality were bending under the weight of his power. "And you, Warden, *are* a fool," Tharion spat. "You cling to this delusion that love can save you, but it will only bring about your destruction. In the end, the stars belong to the void. They always have."

The darkness surged forward again, a tidal wave of malice that threatened to consume them both. Isolde could feel it, the overwhelming weight of his presence, the way it twisted and gnawed at her, pulling her under. For a brief moment, doubt gripped her. She had given so much—sacrificed so much—and yet, here she was, facing a darkness so vast it felt impossible to overcome.

But then she looked at Lior.

His light was flickering, yes—but it was *there*. It was still there, deep within him, even if it was weak. And it wasn't just Lior's light that mattered—it was theirs. *Together*, they were stronger than the darkness. *Together*, they could heal the stars.

A surge of power rushed through her, an undeniable wave of light that radiated from her heart. The stars. Their love. The bond they shared—it was *everything*. And she would not let it be undone. Not by Tharion. Not by the darkness.

Isolde pushed forward, pulling Lior with her, and the stars around them began to flare, brighter and brighter. The bond between them flared to life like an unstoppable fire, expanding outward. The Abyss seemed to push back, the darkness recoiling for the first time, unable to contain the overwhelming light.

"Lior!" Isolde cried, her voice carrying through the surge of energy, through the shattering darkness. "We can do this. Together!"

His light flickered again, weaker, but the pulse of their bond strengthened, becoming a single, unified force. And as they stood there, hand in hand, surrounded by the ever-growing surge of starlight, Isolde knew what they had to do.

"We end this," she said, her voice filled with a power she had never known she possessed. "Now."

Lior's gaze met hers, his eyes bright with the remnants of his fading light. "Together," he whispered. "For the stars."

And with that final whisper, they let the light surge forward.

It was like a thousand stars bursting into existence all at once—a single, overwhelming pulse of pure energy that shot through the Abyss like a spear of light. The darkness shuddered, recoiling, twisting in agony as the light tore through it. Tharion screamed, a sound so full of pain that it shook the very universe itself, but the light—*their* light—burned through him, unrelenting and pure.

The darkness began to unravel, its form dissipating like smoke in the wind. Tharion's figure twisted and writhed in the brilliant surge of light, but he was no match for the combined power of Isolde and Lior. The light engulfed him, suffocating him, burning away the corruption that had consumed him for so long.

"No," Tharion gasped, his voice filled with disbelief as his form began to disintegrate. "You... cannot..."

But his words faded, lost in the blinding radiance that surrounded them. The stars themselves flared to life again, their light growing stronger, more vibrant as the darkness was finally eradicated.

For a moment, there was nothing but the light—the overwhelming, all-encompassing brilliance that filled the universe, the stars burning brighter than they ever had before.

But even as the darkness was vanquished, Isolde felt the strain of their bond. The light that had once burned so bright now flickered again, weak and fragile. She could feel Lior's presence fading, his energy slipping away.

"No," she whispered, fear rising in her chest once more. "Lior, no. Please. Don't—"

But his form was already flickering, and his presence—his light—was dimming.

Isolde's heart shattered as she reached for him, her fingers trembling as she tried to hold on to him, to the fading light. "Please, Lior," she cried, her voice broken. "I can't lose you. Not now. Not after all we've been through."

Lior's eyes met hers, a faint, fading smile curling on his lips. "I'm sorry," he whispered, his voice soft, barely audible. "But this was always the price. The stars… they needed me. But… it's your turn now, Isolde. *You* are the light now."

With those final words, Lior's form flickered one last time, and then—like the dying embers of a once-brilliant flame—his light was gone. The bond between them snapped, and the stars, despite their newfound brilliance, seemed to grow dimmer, their light hollow.

Isolde stood there, trembling, her hands still reaching out toward the space where Lior had been. The stars around her flickered again, and she realized, with the deepest ache in her chest, that the universe had won—*but at what cost?*

She had given everything. She had saved the stars.

But now, she was left with only the silence.

The silence and the stars.

And with that silence, Isolde knew one thing for certain: her fight had not ended. It had only just begun.

Ten

The Battle of Hearts

The universe, once so beautifully ordered, now seemed to shudder under the weight of its impending destruction. The stars, the ancient sentinels of existence, trembled in their celestial prison, their once-pure light flickering as if uncertain of its own survival. The very fabric of the cosmos seemed fragile, stretching thin under the ever-growing shadow of Tharion. His presence, a vortex of raw, consuming darkness, loomed larger with each passing second.

Isolde's heart thundered in her chest as she faced him. The fallen star, the harbinger of corruption and despair, stood before them, a towering figure wreathed in darkness, his eyes burning with the intensity of a thousand dying stars. The weight of his power pressed down on her, suffocating her every breath, and the air around her crackled with an ominous energy.

Beside her, Lior stood, his form flickering with the faintest remnants of light. His once-strong radiance was now reduced to a weak pulse, flickering like a candle caught in a windstorm. His injuries were grave—she could feel it in the way his hand trembled as he reached for hers. The bond between them, once so strong, now wavered, flickering like the dying embers of a fire. Isolde's own strength was draining, the energy she had borrowed from the stars to bind her fate with Lior now ebbing away, leaving her vulnerable.

"Isolde," Lior's voice was a strained whisper, barely audible over the sound of the encroaching darkness. "I—I can feel it. The connection between us…it's fading. You… You have to…" He winced, a jagged breath escaping him. "You have to stop him. Please."

Her heart broke as she looked at him. This was not the vibrant, radiant star she had fallen in love with. This was a dying light, a flickering shadow. And yet, despite the pain, despite the weakening of his form, there was a quiet determination in his eyes—a will to fight, a desire to protect not just her but everything they had both fought for.

The darkness around them roiled, an oppressive force that seemed to tighten with every passing moment. Tharion's cold laugh echoed through the vast expanse, a sound like breaking glass. "You're too late," he sneered, his voice reverberating in the very core of Isolde's being. "You've already lost."

Isolde's eyes locked on him, her hand tightening around Lior's. She could feel him slipping away, his light struggling to remain. But there was no time for despair, no room for fear. The choice was clear: fight, or lose everything.

"Not yet," Isolde said, her voice low and resolute. "We're not finished. Not while we still have a breath to fight with."

Tharion's eyes glowed with a malevolent light as he stepped forward, his form shifting like liquid shadow. "You think you can stop me with your love?" he asked, his tone mocking. "You think your bond can overcome the very power of the void? I was once like you, a protector of the stars. But the universe has betrayed me. And now, I will reshape it in my image."

Isolde could feel the truth of his words, the remnants of the star he had once been flickering through the blackness that now consumed him. There had been a time when Tharion had been a protector, just like her. A star who had stood at the front lines against the darkness, a celestial guardian. But somewhere along the way, something had snapped. Jealousy. Anger. The belief that he could control the stars, that their light could be bent to his will. The same darkness that now threatened to consume everything she loved.

"We won't let you," Isolde said, stepping forward, her voice rising with conviction. The stars, despite their flickering light, still burned within her, and the bond she shared with Lior was a flame that refused to be extinguished. "We will not let you destroy everything."

Tharion's laughter echoed again, darker this time, like a death knell. "You are nothing, Warden. You've bound yourself to a dying star. You've chosen to be part of something that is already fading. How do you think this will end? There is no future for you, no salvation. Only the void."

The darkness around them grew, a tangible, suffocating force that seemed to reach out and touch her very soul. Isolde's breath caught in her throat, but she refused to let it show. She could not falter now. Not when everything depended on her.

Lior's hand tightened around hers, his pulse weak but steady. "Isolde," he whispered again, his voice barely more than a breath. "You have to… you have to end this. I can feel myself fading. But… if you make the choice, if you choose to save the stars, I'll be with you. Always."

Her heart wrenched at the pain in his voice, but she knew what had to be done. She had already given everything to save him. Now, the universe itself demanded more. The stars themselves demanded more.

"I won't lose you, Lior," Isolde said, her voice firm, though her heart was breaking. She could feel the weight of their bond, the thread of light that connected them, but it was slipping. She had to find the strength to hold on, not just for him but for everything. For the universe. For the stars.

The darkness swirled around them, the very air thick with the pressure of Tharion's power. "You don't understand, Isolde," Tharion taunted, his voice slithering through the air like poison. "Your love won't save you. Your bond won't stop me. You're a fleeting moment in the eternal darkness. The stars were never meant to survive."

"Then I'll fight for them," Isolde said, stepping forward, her voice a roar of defiance. "I'll fight for every star, every breath of light, every moment of beauty that's worth saving. You don't own the stars, Tharion. You never did."

With a final surge of energy, Isolde reached out to Lior, her hands trembling as she touched the flickering flame of his light. The bond between them flared briefly, then flickered again. She could feel the pull of the darkness surrounding them, trying to sever the connection, but she refused to let it happen.

"Lior, stay with me," she whispered, her voice a plea, even as her heart broke with the weight of the choice she was about to make. "We're stronger than this. Together, we can stop him."

Lior's form flickered once more, and for a moment, it seemed as though he might slip completely into the darkness. His light was so faint now, barely visible against the tide of shadows, but his eyes locked with hers, and in them, she saw something that made her heart ache. A quiet acceptance. A love that was willing to sacrifice everything to save the stars.

"I'll fight with you," Lior said, his voice barely a whisper, but it carried more strength than Isolde had ever heard from him. "You *are* the light now, Isolde. And together, we will save everything."

The stars above them seemed to respond, a flicker of brilliance that brightened their path. The connection between them, weak as it was, surged with a final, desperate pulse of power, and Isolde knew what she had to do.

With a cry, she reached out to the dying light of Lior, her heart pounding as the stars themselves seemed to align. The power of their bond flared to life, and the light of the stars surged within her, their energy flowing through her veins like fire. But there was a price.

She could feel it in the very depths of her soul. This was the moment of reckoning. The universe demanded sacrifice, and she was the one who would have to pay it.

"Isolde!" Lior cried, his voice thick with desperation as he felt the pull of her energy growing. "No! You don't have to—"

But it was too late.

The moment her power surged forward, Isolde felt the rift between her and Lior widen. The connection between them, once so strong, began to crack, the very fabric of their love straining as the energy she was channeling pulled at her soul. It was a choice that would sever everything, but it was a choice she had to make. To save Lior, to save the stars, she would have to let go.

"Stay with me," she whispered, her tears falling as she focused every ounce of her strength on the stars, on Lior, on the love that had brought her this far. The darkness seemed to howl around them, but the light—their light—was stronger now. It burned bright, and it tore through the Abyss, cutting through the shadows like a blade.

But as the darkness screeched, something shifted. The connection between Isolde and Lior snapped completely. She could feel him fading from her, his light becoming a distant memory, and the universe seemed to tremble under the weight of their final battle. His presence—a part of her—was slipping away, and the fear, the heartbreak, gripped her with a ferocity she had never known.

Tharion's laugh echoed around them, louder now, his power intensifying as he reached into the very fabric of reality. "You think you can fight this?" he snarled, his form shifting and pulsating with shadows. "You think you can stop me with your love?"

Isolde's chest tightened, and for the briefest of moments, she felt her soul unraveling under the weight of his words. But then, she remembered. She remembered the stars. She remembered Lior.

"I will fight," she whispered, her voice steady despite the agony tearing through her. "I will fight for *us*."

And with that, she drove the light forward.

The darkness screamed.

The stars burned brighter than they ever had before.

And Isolde's heart shattered as she let the light consume them all.

The light surged forward, blinding in its brilliance, a roaring force that tore through the fabric of the Abyss, unraveling the shadows that Tharion had wrought. Isolde felt her very essence burning, as though every star in the universe had focused its energy through her body. The universe itself seemed to hum in response, the celestial balance quivering under the raw power of her will.

But with that surge came a deep, crushing emptiness. Her heart, once tethered so firmly to Lior's, felt as though it had been wrenched from her chest. The bond they shared was faltering, slipping through her fingers like grains of sand in a violent storm. She reached for him, reaching for the fading echo of his light, but it was as though the space between them had become an insurmountable chasm. His light, once so vibrant, was now a distant flicker—barely a spark in the overwhelming darkness.

Lior's voice—weak, almost imperceptible—echoed in her mind. *You've given everything, Isolde... don't give up.*

His words seemed to be a distant memory, but the pain in them was sharp, more real than anything she had ever felt. She had made the decision. She had chosen the stars. But the cost of that decision was greater than she had ever imagined.

Tharion's laughter cut through her thoughts, his voice dark and cruel. "You think you've won? You think your light can save the universe? It was always going to end this way. You're just a fleeting spark, Warden. You will burn out just like the rest. You cannot fight the inevitable."

The shadows around them surged forward again, as if they could smell her weakness, as if they were trying to consume her once and for all. The air crackled with his power, the very space around them warping as if reality itself was bending in response to Tharion's will. Isolde could feel her energy draining rapidly, her connection to Lior flickering with each passing moment.

"No…" Isolde breathed, her voice barely audible against the crushing weight of the darkness. She couldn't let him win. Not like this. Not when they had come so far.

With every fiber of her being, she summoned the last of her strength, pushing forward with the power of their bond, the energy of the stars coursing through her. She couldn't stop now. She couldn't let Tharion's darkness take everything they had fought for. The stars—they needed her. *Lior needed her.*

She turned to face him, her eyes filled with sorrow, but also with something else—a deep, burning determination. "I won't let you win, Tharion. I will not let you consume everything."

The darkness around them writhed in response, the very air shuddering under the force of his power. Tharion's form seemed to ripple, and for a brief moment, the twisted figure of a star—flickering with a memory of brightness—emerged from the shadow. But it was not the light of the stars that Isolde saw. It was the void. The abyss that had consumed him. The rage. The jealousy. The anger.

"You cannot stop me," Tharion hissed. "I will *remake* the universe in my image. I will bring it to its knees, and you— *you*—will watch as everything burns."

The energy between them surged again, a wave of power that threatened to tear her apart. Isolde's body trembled, her connection to Lior now a flickering ember in the storm of energy, but she couldn't let go. Not now. Not when the universe was on the line.

She could feel it, the pull of darkness trying to unravel her, trying to take her. She had sacrificed so much, given so much, but in this final moment, she had one thing left to fight for.

Lior.

Isolde's eyes found his form, dim but still there, still clinging to life. His light flickered faintly, but she could feel the remnants of their bond, the echo of his soul, still there. *Don't let go,* she thought fiercely, reaching for him with everything she had left.

Lior's voice came to her, so soft she almost couldn't hear it. *Isolde... it's okay. You've done more than I ever dreamed. You've fought for everything we are, everything the stars represent. Now, let me go. Let me fade. It's... it's time.*

"No..." Isolde's voice cracked, her chest tight with pain. "I won't let you go. Not like this. Not after everything we've been through. I can't lose you, Lior."

Tharion's shadow loomed over them, his laugh echoing, mocking, filled with malice. "It's already done. You can't save him. You can't save anyone. Your love... it means nothing here."

The darkness surged forward again, a tidal wave of hatred, but this time, Isolde did not falter. She reached out with everything inside of her, summoning the light—the power of their connection. She could feel the stars reaching out to her, their energy merging with hers as the cosmic force surged through her veins. The pull of Tharion's darkness threatened to crush her, but her love for Lior was stronger.

"No," she whispered, her voice a low, fierce defiance. "*Love is everything.*"

With that, the energy she had called upon exploded outward, a surge of pure starlight that erupted from her like a burst of fire. The darkness recoiled, screaming in fury as the light clashed against it. For a moment, there was nothing but the sound of their wills fighting against each other, the cracking, splintering force of light pushing back against the consuming void.

The stars themselves seemed to roar to life, their light growing, burning brighter and brighter until the void could no longer resist. But even as the light surged, Isolde felt the strain—the weight of the darkness still trying to pull her under, to shatter the connection she had with Lior.

"Lior!" she cried, her voice breaking. "Please… don't fade. Stay with me. Stay with the stars."

The moment she spoke, she felt it—the bond that connected them flare to life, a pulse of warmth in the cold void. Lior's light flickered again, and for a moment, she thought she had lost him. But then, she felt him reach for her, feel his hand in hers, a faint warmth in the endless cold.

"I'm here," Lior whispered, his voice faint but steady. "I'm still here. And I'll never leave you. Not in the stars, not in the darkness. Together. Always."

The power between them surged once more, stronger than before, and this time, it was *unstoppable*. Isolde focused everything on their bond, on the love she had for him, on the strength of the stars and the universe they were fighting for. With one final, explosive surge of energy, the light they had summoned tore through the darkness like a blade, rending the void apart.

Tharion screamed, a howl of agony as the light consumed him, burning through the layers of darkness that had corrupted him. The shadows around him cracked, shattered by the force of the starlight, and for the first time, Isolde saw the man Tharion had once been—the protector, the star.

And then, he was gone.

The darkness unraveled, the void dissipating like smoke in the wind, leaving only the remnants of the cosmic balance that had nearly been lost. The stars above them flared to life once more, their light returning to the heavens.

But Isolde could feel the cost. The energy she had expended, the force of their bond, the love she had given to protect Lior and the stars—it had drained her. Her body trembled, her vision swimming with the aftershock of the battle. She could feel the emptiness threatening to swallow her whole.

And yet… Lior's light still remained. It was faint, barely there, but it *was* there.

Lior's voice, weak but steady, echoed in her mind: *We've done it, Isolde. We've saved the stars. Together, we've saved the universe.*

Isolde sank to her knees, the exhaustion from the battle threatening to overtake her. She could feel the weight of their victory, the cost of their love, and for the briefest of moments, she allowed herself to close her eyes. She had won. They had won.

And yet, the price had been so high.

As her mind swirled with exhaustion, Lior's light pulsed weakly, his form flickering, and she knew then that the true battle—one that would define the fate of their love—was only just beginning.

Eleven

The Warden's Choice

The air in the Tower of the Stars grew thick with an unnatural stillness, like the calm before a violent storm. Isolde stood at the edge of the vast, open space, gazing out at the stars. Once, they had been so beautiful—beacons of light that illuminated the universe with their ancient glow, steady and eternal. But now, they flickered and dimmed, fading into the abyss that threatened to swallow them whole.

Her heart felt like lead in her chest, heavy with the weight of the decision she was about to make. Every pulse of light from the stars seemed to call out to her, urging her to take the final step. She could feel it deep within her soul, the deep, painful connection that linked her to Lior. The bond between them had grown in strength and intensity, but it had come at a price. The stars had borne witness to their love, their struggles, and now the final act of that love would either save them or destroy everything they held dear.

Lior was dying. She could feel it in every beat of her heart. His light—so once so powerful—was now weak, flickering in and out like a dying ember. The darkness that had consumed Tharion was beginning to take hold of him too, slowly draining the life force from his celestial being. Isolde could see the faint outline of him beside her, his form growing dimmer with each passing moment.

A soft, anguished breath left her lips as she turned toward him. His eyes met hers, filled with a quiet sorrow. His pain was visible, the agony of someone who had given up everything for love, only to see that love slowly slipping away.

"Isolde," Lior whispered, his voice barely a breath against the roaring silence that surrounded them. "You don't have to do this. I've already… I've already lived my purpose. You've already given so much for me, for the stars. I don't want you to…"

His voice trailed off, but Isolde knew what he was trying to say. He didn't want her to sacrifice herself—not for him, not for the stars. But she had already made up her mind.

"I can't lose you," she said softly, stepping closer to him. She could feel the familiar warmth of his fading light brushing against her skin, a gentle reminder of the bond they had forged. Her fingers trembled as she reached out to him, her hand hovering just above his, feeling the delicate thread of their connection. "I won't let the universe fall because of my hesitation. I made a promise. A promise to the stars… and to you."

Lior closed his eyes, a pained breath escaping his lips. "If you choose to do this, Isolde, you'll lose everything. You'll never be the Warden again. You'll lose your immortality. The stars… they won't be the same."

"I don't care," she replied, her voice unwavering. "I will be with you. Always. I would rather fade with you, Lior, than live without you."

The silence stretched between them, thick and heavy, and the weight of her words hung in the air. She knew the consequences of what she was about to do. It wasn't just her life she was offering up—it was the entire essence of her being. The Heart of the Tower was the only place where the ritual could take place, the only place where she could bind her soul to Lior's, tethering her existence to his. But the cost of that ritual was greater than she could have ever imagined.

The Heart of the Tower—a mystical, ancient artifact that had existed since the dawn of time—held unimaginable power. But it was a power that came with a terrible price. Those who called upon it risked their very existence. Those who dared to use it often vanished, leaving behind only traces of their power, scattered across the stars.

"Isolde," Lior murmured, his voice full of both love and desperation. "You don't have to do this. We've fought together. We've already won. You've already done enough."

But Isolde's resolve was as unyielding as the stars themselves. She knew what had to be done. She had already given so much. Her heart, her soul, and now… she was willing to give everything. The universe had been her charge. The stars had always been her duty. And now, she would protect them, even at the cost of her own immortality.

"I've made my choice, Lior," she said, her voice soft but firm. "I won't leave you. Not now. Not when I can still do something."

Lior's eyes shone with unshed tears, his light flickering more erratically now. "Isolde… I love you. More than the stars themselves. But this… it isn't worth it."

"I don't care," she said softly, her eyes filled with unspeakable sorrow. "If I can't be with you, I don't want to exist in a world without the stars."

Her voice cracked on the last word, and Lior's form faltered. She could feel the weight of his energy slipping away, but she pushed the pain aside. She had already made her decision.

With a final glance at Lior, she turned away, her feet carrying her toward the Heart of the Tower. The ancient artifact sat in the center of the chamber, glowing faintly with a pulsing, ethereal light. The energy around it thrummed like a heartbeat, a constant reminder of the power it held. It was both beautiful and terrifying.

Isolde closed her eyes, drawing in a shaky breath. She could feel the weight of the universe on her shoulders now, the magnitude of what she was about to do crashing down on her with full force. Every breath felt like it was coming from someone else, someone who no longer existed. The stars—those ancient beacons of hope—were fading, their light slipping further and further away as the darkness continued to claw at the edges of the universe. And it was her fault. It was her duty. She was the Warden of the Stars, and it was her responsibility to keep the balance intact.

But balance came with a price.

And she was ready to pay it.

Stepping up to the Heart of the Tower, she extended her hand. The cool surface of the Heart pulsed under her fingertips, its ancient power flaring briefly before settling into a soft, steady hum. Isolde closed her eyes, drawing on the energy of the Heart. Her mind swirled with a thousand images—the stars, the universe, the lives that depended on the delicate balance she had sworn to protect. Her heart, too, beat in time with the pulse of the Heart, and she felt something shift deep within her. The magic was rising, building in her veins, a sharp, intoxicating force that filled her with both fear and awe.

"Isolde…" Lior's voice cracked in the distance, but she couldn't look back. The choice had been made. She would not allow the stars to fall. She would not allow the universe to collapse under the weight of Tharion's darkness.

The magic surged, and she felt herself being pulled into a vast, void-like space—a place beyond time and existence. The very fabric of the universe stretched thin around her, the stars now just tiny specks of light in an infinite darkness.

The connection between her and Lior pulsed faintly in her mind, distant but still there, like a thread pulling her forward. Her heart beat faster as the ritual began, her soul beginning to fuse with Lior's. The magic of the Heart flooded her, coursing through her like fire, binding her to Lior in a way that transcended time, space, and even existence itself. She could feel him, the warmth of his light flickering just beyond the reach of her grasp.

But with that warmth came a deep, gnawing emptiness. The stars, the light, the love—they were all fading. And as she bound herself to him, she felt herself unraveling.

The magic was too much. The cost was too high.

"I'm sorry, Lior," she whispered, her voice breaking as the power surged through her, consuming her, pulling at her very soul. The darkness was trying to tear them apart, trying to pull them into the void. She could feel it. The final thread between them was slipping, fading, but she would not let go. She would not leave him to fade in the darkness alone.

The stars screamed.

Isolde's breath became shallow, her vision swimming as the light and dark warred within her. The universe itself trembled, the very laws of time and space bending under the weight of her sacrifice. She could feel the end coming—the end of her life, the end of her immortality, the end of everything she had ever known. But in the distance, just beyond the chaos, she saw it: the glow of the stars, faint but steady. They were alive. They were still there.

And with that, Isolde knew that she had made the right choice.

Her soul was fading, but the stars were safe.

Lior's voice, soft and filled with love, echoed through the growing darkness. *We're together, Isolde. Always.*

And then, with the final pulse of magic, the universe began to realign.

The balance had been restored.

And Isolde's light, along with Lior's, flickered into eternity.

The universe hummed softly in the aftermath of the ritual. The blackness that had enveloped everything, that had choked the light from the stars, began to recede, slowly, like a tide pulled back by an unseen force. But Isolde could barely feel the change. She was slipping away, her body and soul fraying at the edges as the immense power of the Heart of the Tower pulsed through her, binding her to Lior in a way she had never imagined.

Her breathing was shallow, ragged, as the magic swirled within her, consuming everything she had been. She could feel it, the very last threads of her immortality unraveling like threads from an ancient tapestry. The stars that had once been her charge now seemed like distant memories, fading just as the light within her faded. Her eyes fluttered open, and she gazed out into the vast expanse of the cosmos, seeing the constellations return to life, their once-weak light now shining strong again, piercing through the remnants of the darkness that had nearly swallowed them all.

But her gaze was unfocused. Her limbs felt heavy, numb. The pulse of the universe, once a familiar rhythm she had felt every moment of her life, now seemed distant and foreign. The connection between her and Lior, that fragile thread of light and warmth, was still there, but it too was waning, the bond now a shadow of what it had once been.

"Lior…" Isolde's voice came out as a whisper, a faint breath that barely reached her own ears. Her hand shook as she extended it towards him, feeling his presence—his light—a distant flicker that seemed to pulse with every beat of her heart. He was still there, still alive, but she could feel him slipping away, just as she was.

She could see him—see his form, dim and flickering, yet somehow still there. But his light, so vibrant and full of life once, was now barely a flicker, like the last ember of a dying fire.

"Isolde…" Lior's voice was weak, broken, but still full of love. "I—I'm sorry."

"No." Isolde's voice broke on the word, her chest aching with the weight of it. "You don't need to apologize. You didn't do anything wrong. I… I chose this. We chose this."

But as she spoke, she knew deep down that it was more than just their choice that had led them here. It was the very fabric of the universe itself that had demanded this price. Her immortality had been sacrificed for the stars. Her very soul was bound to his, to the light of the stars, and she could feel it slipping through her fingers like sand in the wind.

"I can't…" she whispered, her voice catching in her throat. She tried to reach for him, her hand trembling as she struggled to stay connected, to feel him near her. The light between them flickered, but it was faint, like the soft glow of a candle in the wind.

Lior's form flickered as well, and his body swayed, the light within him dimming more rapidly with each passing moment. His eyes, once filled with hope and fire, were now clouded with pain and sorrow. "Isolde… I'm sorry I couldn't—"

"No," she said again, her voice firm despite the weakness creeping into her limbs. "You gave everything. We both did. We've done more than anyone could ever ask of us. We gave our hearts… our lives… our love. And now, the stars are safe. They are shining again."

She could feel the universe around them slowly healing. The stars—once dim and on the verge of extinction—began to burn brighter, their light returning, though still faint. She could hear them whispering, their voices soft and distant, like a chorus singing a song of rebirth. She had done it. She had saved them.

But the cost was everything.

"Lior…" Her voice faltered again as her hands gripped his, the last of her strength fading with the effort. "I will always love you. Always. Even if I fade into the stars, even if my light is gone, I'll be with you. We'll always be one."

Tears filled her eyes as she looked at him, unable to bear the thought of leaving him, of the bond between them breaking. But she could feel it. The bond was breaking, unraveling. She was slipping away, and Lior—his light—was growing dimmer.

Isolde's heart clenched painfully in her chest, the agony of knowing that she had made this choice but now could not bear the consequences. She had sacrificed everything for love—everything she had ever known. And now, she was fading into the very stars she had sworn to protect.

And yet… despite the overwhelming pain, there was a quiet peace in her heart. The universe was still alive. The stars still burned. And their love, their bond, was eternal, even if the light within them dimmed.

"Isolde," Lior whispered, his voice cracking. His eyes, full of sorrow, met hers one last time, and the flicker of his light seemed to burn brighter for just a moment. "I will never forget you. I will never forget *us*."

The stars seemed to respond to his words, their light brightening, their warmth swelling in the cosmos. It was as if they were sending him their final blessings. The energy of the universe was shifting, re-aligning itself with the balance they had fought so desperately to preserve.

Isolde closed her eyes, her breath becoming shallow as the last remnants of her power slipped away. She could feel herself fading, her consciousness slipping from her body, but she was at peace. She had made the right choice. They had made the right choice.

With a final, lingering thought, she allowed herself to let go. The universe had been saved. And her love for Lior, for the stars, would endure beyond the boundaries of time and space. Her heart was no longer bound to her mortal body. It was scattered across the stars, bound to the very fabric of the universe itself.

Lior's light flickered one last time, then—just as Isolde felt herself slipping into the eternal abyss of starlight—his presence surged, filling the space around her, his warmth flooding her very soul.

And then… everything went quiet.

The stars were alive.

But the Warden of the Stars had gone.

The cosmic expanse, now healed and whole once more, stood silent in the wake of Isolde's sacrifice. The universe, once teetering on the edge of destruction, had found its balance again, thanks to the love of two souls willing to give up everything for the light of the stars.

And in the silence, there was a peace. A peace that would echo across time and space for all eternity.

The stars—alive, bright, and eternal—burned on.

And though Isolde had faded from the world of the living, her legacy remained: in the stars. In the very heart of the universe, where light and love never truly die.

Forever.

Twelve

The Star's Last Breath

The void was silent, save for the faint, mournful hum of the stars. Their light, though now restored, felt fragile, like a candle barely holding against a howling wind. Isolde's light had faded, leaving nothing but the empty space where it once burned, her final breath a whisper against the vastness of the cosmos. Lior stood at the edge of the universe, staring at the spot where her presence had once been, his heart heavy with a grief that tore through him like a storm.

Isolde was gone. The weight of her sacrifice crashed against him in relentless waves. The stars—those very stars she had fought so hard to protect—were now burning as a tribute to the love they had shared, their once-glorious light now dimmed with her passing.

He had watched her fade, his hand outstretched, trembling as he reached for her. She had given everything for the universe. But now, with her light extinguished, the universe felt hollow.

Her absence was more than just the loss of a celestial being. It was the loss of *her*—the woman who had been his anchor in the storm, the one whose love had sparked a fire within him that no darkness could quench.

"Isolde," he whispered, his voice breaking, the words leaving his lips as nothing more than a desperate plea. The stars above seemed to flicker in answer, a mournful pulse, but it wasn't enough. It would never be enough.

The universe was silent.

Lior's hands shook as he closed his eyes, the weight of his loss pressing down on him like an unbearable burden. He had never known such a crushing emptiness. And yet, deep within his chest, there was still a flicker. A faint, fragile spark of the light they had shared.

"No." Lior's voice was firm as his eyes opened again, fixating on the stars above him. The flickering light of the heavens danced in the darkness like embers caught in the wind. "I won't let this be the end."

The stars. He had always known their power. He had always been one with them, their light his life force. And now, in this moment of desperation, he would draw upon that power. He would do anything, anything to bring her back.

He stepped forward, his feet light upon the celestial ground, and his heart burned with a fierce resolve. Lior extended his arms toward the heavens, feeling the energy of the universe gather in his body, swirling within him, alive and electric. His skin tingled with the raw power of the stars, their energy coursing through him like fire, like the very essence of life itself. But this power—it wasn't enough to save her. It would never be enough to undo what had already been done.

But he couldn't accept that. Not yet.

She can't be gone. She can't be.

His breath came in short, desperate bursts as he closed his eyes and began to channel the stars' energy, pulling it into himself. The pulse of their light grew stronger, more intense, flooding his body with warmth and strength. But the cost of this was becoming more apparent with every passing moment. The stars themselves seemed to recoil, their light dimming as Lior's energy grew. He could feel it—the strain, the exhaustion. This was a desperate act, one that could cost him his life. But he didn't care. Not anymore.

"Isolde," he whispered again, the words a prayer, a plea. His heart was racing in his chest as he reached out, his energy now fully merged with the stars. The light was within him, coursing through his veins, and yet it felt like something was slipping away, just beyond his grasp. "I will not let you fade into the darkness. Not like this."

The cosmos above him trembled.

He could feel the pulse of the stars, each one beating like a heart. They were calling to him, urging him to do this, but they were also warning him. This was not a power to be wielded lightly. If he channeled too much, if he pressed too far, he would tear apart the very fabric of the universe. The balance of the stars had already been shattered once, and now, with Isolde's sacrifice, it was teetering on the edge of collapse.

But in that moment, Lior knew—he could feel it in every fiber of his being—that he had to try.

And so, with a final, desperate cry, he let go.

A pulse of blinding light exploded from him, an overwhelming surge of celestial energy that ripped through the heavens. The stars above him screamed, their voices rising in unison, a chorus of pain and joy and sorrow. The energy pulsed outward, a wave of raw, untamed power that sent ripples through the cosmos. It was as though the universe itself was responding to his plea.

For a moment, the stars burned brighter than they ever had before, their light so fierce that it swallowed the darkness. But even in that brilliance, Lior could feel the pull of the void, the abyss that threatened to consume everything. It was fighting back, clawing at the light with a force so great that it shook the very core of the universe.

"Lior…" Isolde's voice, faint but clear, echoed through the void, like a whisper carried on the wind. Her presence, though weak, was still there, still alive within him. The bond between them was not severed completely, and even as the energy surged, he could feel her—a faint pulse of light, a fading heartbeat.

"Don't give up," she whispered, the words trembling in his mind, as if they were being pulled from her very soul. "You're… you're everything to me, Lior. You've always been."

His heart ached as the light surged again, tearing through him like fire. The pain was unbearable, and he could feel the very fabric of his being being stretched to its limits. His energy, drawn from the stars, was running thin. But he couldn't stop. Not when she was still there, lingering at the edges of his consciousness.

"Please…" Lior gasped, his voice barely audible. "Stay with me. Stay with the stars."

But the void was closing in. The shadows were relentless, and the stars seemed to flicker once more, their light dimming. Lior's own energy was waning, and his body—his celestial form—was becoming weak, the power within him being drained by the very act he had set into motion.

"I can't hold on much longer," he whispered, his breath labored. "Not without you."

The pulse of light from his body grew weaker, and the darkness inched closer.

Suddenly, a figure appeared in the swirling chaos—a presence so familiar, so impossibly distant. Isolde.

Her form shimmered in and out of existence, her light faint, but still there. Lior's breath caught in his chest as he saw her—her eyes locked onto his, filled with both love and sorrow.

"Isolde," he whispered, his voice raw with emotion. His soul surged toward her, reaching out for the warmth of her light, the light that had once been so bright. But the distance between them was vast, stretching farther with every moment. She was fading, slipping away.

"I'm not gone," she said, her voice soft and comforting. But the weariness in her words made it clear that she was struggling to hold on. "But you must save yourself, Lior. You must—"

"I won't let you go," he interrupted, his voice breaking, the words desperate. "Not after everything we've been through. I won't lose you. You gave everything for me, for the stars. I won't—"

"You have to," she said, her voice firm now, though the strain in it was clear. "Lior, listen to me. You can't sacrifice yourself for me. You have to survive. You have to save the stars. That's what you were born to do."

His heart shattered at the words, the weight of them pressing down on him with the force of a thousand collapsing stars. How could he let her go? How could he *live* without her?

"I love you, Isolde," he whispered, his voice barely audible. "I always will. You are the stars. You are everything."

Her light flickered, a faint, fragile pulse, and for a moment,

Lior thought he had lost her completely. But then, she was there again, her form flickering like the last remaining ember of a dying flame. She smiled softly, her eyes full of that same love that had carried them through everything.

"I'll be with you, Lior. Always."

And with those final words, she faded. Her light, once so radiant, slipped away into the depths of the cosmos, her soul now bound to the very fabric of the stars themselves.

Lior felt it—felt the very essence of her leave him. The bond that had connected them, so strong, so unbreakable, was severed, and the empty void left in its wake threatened to swallow him whole.

But Isolde was right. She had given everything for the stars. And now, it was his turn.

He stood alone in the silence, the energy of the stars surrounding him, their light growing brighter once more as the darkness finally began to recede. The cosmos, though scarred, was healing. And though his heart was broken, his soul torn in two, he knew that the stars still burned because of their love.

With a final, mournful breath, Lior reached into the depths of his power and let it surge through him once more. It was the last of his strength—the last of the light he had left to give.

The stars burned brighter than they ever had before.

Lior's heart beat like a war drum, the pounding echo of desperation and resolve. The universe had been fractured, bent to the will of darkness. But now, it was on the brink of mending itself, all because of him. Because of their love.

The pain in his chest intensified. Isolde was gone—her light had faded, slipping away like dust into the wind. And yet, her presence still lingered within him. He could feel her, a faint pulse, as though she were just beyond the veil of existence. She had become part of the stars themselves, her soul scattered through the cosmic expanse, her light now part of the very fabric of the universe.

Lior closed his eyes, swallowing the rising lump in his throat. He could not mourn her yet—not when there was still work to be done. Not when the very fabric of the universe was teetering on the edge of collapse.

He stood at the center of the cosmic expanse, alone, with nothing but the faint glow of the stars flickering around him. His form—once bright, a beacon of celestial power—was now fragile, the light within him dimming with each passing second. The energy he had called upon to restore balance had drained him. His body was worn, brittle as if the very core of his being had been stripped away.

But there was still something left. A pulse, weak but present. His connection to the stars was still alive, though it flickered like a candle in the wind.

The cosmos around him seemed to sway with the weight of the task at hand. The balance had been restored, yes, but at what cost? Isolde was gone. And Lior was no longer whole. He was now the last protector of the stars, but the price of that duty had been steep. He had lost the love of his life, the one person who had shared this journey with him.

And yet, he couldn't stop. He couldn't let the stars fade into oblivion. He couldn't let her sacrifice be in vain.

Lior clenched his fists, his knuckles white. He reached outward, feeling the faint pulse of the stars, the remnants of their power. They called to him, whispered to him, urging him to hold on. He would not let them down. He had to fight.

A figure appeared before him—distant at first, a shadow on

the horizon. Then, it took form.

Tharion.

The fallen star was no longer a towering figure of darkness and malice. His form, while still shrouded in shadow, seemed to flicker in and out of existence like an apparition. The once-overwhelming power he had wielded was now fractured, a reflection of his broken soul. Tharion's eyes glowed faintly, no longer burning with the intensity they once had, but dim and weak, much like Lior's own fading light.

"You…" Tharion's voice rasped as he stepped closer, his presence filling the space with a cold, oppressive energy. "You think you've won? The stars are still weak. Their light is fragile, Lior. You've destroyed me, but you haven't restored what you've lost. You haven't won."

Lior's heart skipped a beat. "You're wrong," he said, his voice hoarse, but filled with conviction. "I *have* won. The stars are alive. The universe is whole again. Your darkness is fading, Tharion. You've lost."

Tharion's laugh was soft, bitter, echoing through the void. "I've lost?" he repeated, his gaze narrowing as he looked at Lior. "I was never trying to win, Lior. I was trying to *understand*." His voice softened, and for a fleeting moment, the bitterness was replaced by something else—something that resembled regret, or perhaps resignation. "You are right. You've won. But I did not fall because I sought power. I fell because I loved the stars too much. And now, look at them. Look at what you've done. They're dying, Lior. Just like I did."

Lior took a step back, his heart aching. Tharion's words hit him hard, more than he wanted to admit. He had *loved* the stars, just like Tharion. He had given his soul to them, just like Isolde had. And now, he was left alone with a universe that had been saved—but at what cost? Isolde was gone. The stars had been saved, but the love that had fueled them… it had burned out.

"No," Lior said, shaking his head as his voice grew more steady. "The stars live because of what Isolde and I did. Her sacrifice was not in vain. And neither will mine be."

Tharion took a step closer, his shadowy form flickering again. "And what is your sacrifice, Lior? You've already lost everything. Your immortality, your love, your purpose. You've given it all for something that was never meant to be saved."

Lior's hands shook with the force of his words. "I have nothing left to lose," he said, his voice quiet but resolute. "But I still have something to give. The stars deserve more than darkness. They deserve to burn brightly, to *live*."

He reached out with his trembling hands, feeling the pulse of the stars again, pulling the last bit of energy from them. His soul began to hum with their energy, the connection between them swelling like the tide before a storm. The universe trembled in response, the delicate balance threatening to collapse once more. But Lior refused to let it.

"I will give everything," he whispered, the words carried away by the wind. "I will sacrifice everything for the stars."

Tharion watched him, his gaze dark and unreadable. "You would sacrifice yourself for them? Even now, after everything? After you've lost her?"

Lior didn't answer. He didn't need to. The energy of the stars was surging through him, filling the space around him with raw power. He could feel it—the weight of the universe, the burden of the stars' existence, pressing down on him. He had always been a protector. He had always been a part of them. And now, with everything on the line, it was his turn to be their final guardian.

He closed his eyes and let the power surge through him, calling upon the very core of the stars. The light inside him flared, pushing back the shadows, the remnants of Tharion's darkness that still clung to the edges of the cosmos. The stars began to shine brighter, their light rekindling with every ounce of strength Lior poured into them. The energy was wild, untamed, and it surged through him like fire.

But it was not enough.

"Lior," Tharion's voice sounded, broken, weak. "It's too late."

The words echoed in Lior's mind, and for a moment, he faltered. Was it too late? Was there any hope for him? For the stars? For the universe? Was everything truly lost?

But as the darkness around them swirled, a faint voice broke through the chaos. Soft, like the whisper of the stars themselves.

Don't give up.

Isolde.

Her voice. Her light. It pulsed through him, stronger than ever before. He could feel her presence, her love, her essence still connected to him, still alive in the heart of the universe.

Together.

And with that final, overwhelming surge of power, Lior released everything he had left. The light of the stars—Isolde's light, his light—rushed outward, a flood of energy that engulfed everything in its path. The darkness recoiled as the light surged forward, shattering the void and banishing the last remnants of Tharion's influence.

The stars exploded in a burst of light, their brilliance unmatched, their radiance brighter than they had ever been before. The universe shook, the very fabric of existence trembling under the sheer force of Lior's will. He had saved them. He had saved the stars.

But as the light surged, Lior felt himself weaken, his form flickering with the last remnants of his strength. He could feel the energy of the stars beginning to fade within him. The connection between them was still there, but it was fragile, like a thread about to snap.

Lior collapsed to his knees, his body trembling as the stars above him burned brighter than they had ever been before. He had given everything for this moment. His love, his light, his very soul. And now, the stars were safe. The universe was safe.

But it had cost him everything.

Thirteen

A Celestial Rebirth

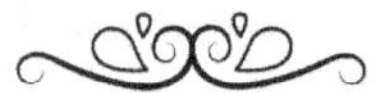

The silence of the universe was suffocating. It stretched out infinitely, an absence so complete that it seemed to echo in every corner of existence. No stars, no planets, no life—nothing moved. It was as though the cosmos itself had drawn a deep breath and held it, suspended between moments of collapse and rebirth.

The battle was over. Tharion, the fallen star, was no more, and with his absence, the darkness that had consumed the heavens began to recede, pulled back like the last remnants of a nightmare. But it was not a victory that felt triumphant. It was a victory laced with the deepest sorrow. The universe had been saved, but at a tremendous cost.

Isolde's light had faded.

The wound left by her sacrifice was still raw, her soul having been bound to Lior's, now intertwined with the stars themselves. In her final act of love and defiance, she had become one with the cosmos, a celestial thread woven into the very fabric of the universe. She was no longer a mere warden of the stars. She was part of them.

Lior stood alone in the vast expanse of the heavens, the remnants of his energy flickering weakly. His form, once radiant, now dimmed like a star on the verge of collapsing. His body was worn, his soul drained, yet his heart—his heart still beat, aching with the absence of the woman he had loved. Isolde was gone. Her essence remained, woven into the light of the stars, but her presence—her warmth, her laughter, her love—was lost to him.

And still, he could feel her.

It wasn't physical. It wasn't a mere presence in the air around him. No. It was deeper than that. Her soul was etched into the fabric of the stars, and with every flicker of their light, he felt her. Her love for him, her promise to never be apart, echoed through the vastness of the cosmos. The universe hummed with her memory, a soft, steady pulse that resonated deep within him.

The stars, once fragile and flickering like dying embers, now blazed brighter than ever before, their light steady and strong. They were alive again, pulsing with the power they had once held. The energy that had once been chaotic, wild, and unstable had calmed, now a force of balance, harmonious and pure. It was as though the stars themselves were breathing again, exhaling a slow, rhythmic pulse that resonated in every corner of the universe.

But with this rebirth came an unbearable weight.

The sky above Lior rippled with the energy of the reborn stars. Their light danced across the expanse, casting ripples of warmth and color, bathing the celestial landscape in a new, shimmering glow. The darkness was gone, yes—but the silence that had followed was profound. It was as though the universe itself was grieving, mourning the sacrifice that had restored it.

Lior stood still, his heart heavy with the emptiness that filled him. His hands trembled at his sides as he reached up, touching his chest where the bond between him and Isolde had once been so strong. The connection was still there, faint but undeniable, like a thread connecting him to the stars themselves. But it was different now. It was distant, stretching further than he could reach.

He could still feel her.

The warmth of her touch, the softness of her voice in his mind. The love they had shared, a love that had defied everything, had transcended the stars themselves. But she was gone. Her body had faded, her form lost to the cosmic winds, but she was still there, embedded in the very essence of the universe. She was part of it now, part of the stars.

"Isolde," Lior whispered, his voice breaking. "You're still here, aren't you?"

A soft breeze blew across the empty expanse of the universe, like a sigh carried on the wind. It was gentle, almost tender, as if the universe itself was comforting him, whispering through the light of the stars. And in that whisper, Lior could hear her—her voice, so soft and distant, but undeniably hers.

I will always be here, Lior. Always. I am the stars now. And so are you.

Her words, though faint, were clear in his mind, and the tears that had longed to escape him finally fell. He closed his eyes and let the warmth of the stars wash over him, feeling the connection between them stir, as though the entire universe was embracing him in its celestial arms. She was still with him.

She would always be with him.

But that wasn't enough.

He needed her here. He needed her by his side.

Lior opened his eyes, staring at the sea of stars above him, their brilliance blinding in its purity. The cosmos stretched out before him, vast and eternal, but it felt empty, devoid of the one thing that had made it whole. *Her.*

He could hear the heartbeat of the universe, its rhythm steady, but beneath that, there was an underlying pulse. Faint, but undeniable. It was the echo of a love that had transcended the boundaries of time, of space, of existence. The stars sang a song of rebirth, of loss, and of love. Isolde had given everything for this, for the stars, for the universe. And now, she had become part of it. Her soul had been woven into the very fabric of the heavens.

Lior sank to his knees, his hands pressed against the stardust below him. He felt the connection between them flare again, a soft, steady pulse, but it was fading. It was slipping away.

"No," he whispered. "I won't let you fade. Not like this."

He reached out, his hands trembling, calling out to the universe. His voice was a soft, desperate plea. "Isolde, please. Come back. Please. I can't… I can't live without you."

The stars above seemed to respond, their light pulsing softly, as though they were listening. But there was no answer, no voice to comfort him. Only the hum of the universe, the rhythm of time passing, the echo of her love in the very stars themselves.

And then, a shift. A sudden, overwhelming surge of energy pulsed through him, through the very fabric of the stars, a shockwave of pure, unrelenting power that sent a tremor through the heavens. The light of the stars flared brighter, a flash so intense it was like the birth of a new star, and then, in that light, he felt it.

Isolde's presence.

Her love.

She was there.

The pulse of energy intensified, rushing through the cosmos like a tidal wave of light, enveloping Lior in its brilliance. His body trembled as the power surged through him, the stars themselves flaring brighter and brighter. He reached out, feeling her light surround him, envelop him in warmth.

And then, a whisper—so faint, so soft.

I'm here, Lior. Always. You never have to let go.

Tears streamed down Lior's face as the light of the stars filled him, wrapping him in a warm embrace. He felt Isolde—felt her love—filling the space around him. She was the stars now. She was the light of the universe. She was part of everything.

But she wasn't gone. She was here, in every flicker of light, every pulse of energy that surged through the universe. He could feel her. She was with him. Always.

The light faded, but the warmth remained, filling his chest with a quiet peace. The universe was healing, its balance restored. The stars had been reborn. They were alive once more, burning brighter than ever, their light now more stable than before.

Lior stood slowly, feeling the weight of everything that had transpired. His body was tired, drained, but his heart felt lighter than it had in what seemed like forever. The universe was still standing, still shining.

And though Isolde was no longer beside him, her love for him—her sacrifice—had ensured that the stars would never fade again.

Her soul was with the stars, woven into the very fabric of existence. Her love was eternal, shining through every flicker of starlight. He could still feel her, her presence lingering in the universe like a gentle touch. And that was enough. That would always be enough.

"Isolde," he whispered once more, his voice filled with reverence. "Thank you."

And as the stars burned brighter above him, he knew that she would always be there—part of the very fabric of the universe, guiding him, watching over him, and loving him from afar. Always. Forever.

The universe was whole again.

And their love—had become eternal.

The universe stretched out before Lior, vast and infinite, its beauty overwhelming in its stillness. The stars, once flickering uncertainly, now burned with a steady, enduring light. The void that had threatened to consume them was now filled with the harmonious pulse of life. The universe had been reborn, its balance restored, but Lior's heart remained heavy.

He stood at the edge of the cosmic expanse, his gaze fixed on the heavens, but his mind was not fully present. His thoughts swirled with the memory of Isolde—her warmth, her love, her sacrifice. She was no longer beside him, no longer tangible, no longer a presence he could touch. Yet she was everywhere. Her essence, her love, her soul had become part of the stars themselves, woven into the fabric of the universe.

Lior closed his eyes, and for a brief, fragile moment, he felt her again. The connection between them pulsed faintly, like the last beating of a heart before it finally fades into silence. He could feel her love surrounding him, a soft, distant warmth that still lingered, even in the absence of her physical form.

"Isolde…" The word escaped his lips in a whisper, almost as if speaking her name would somehow bring her back to him. But the universe responded only with silence. Her presence, now a part of the stars, could not be returned to him.

The cosmos had been restored, but the cost had been everything. The stars burned brightly above him, their light steady and eternal, but the universe felt emptier than ever. The love that had once burned so brightly between him and Isolde had not been extinguished; it had simply been transformed. It lived on in the stars, in the very core of existence, but it was no longer something he could reach out and touch. Her sacrifice had left an indelible mark on the heavens.

He stepped forward, his body weary but still moving, still propelled by the faint echo of her love. He had been reborn alongside the stars, his connection to them stronger than it had ever been. But it was a bittersweet transformation. He would live on, as a star does, but he could never forget the price that had been paid. The warmth of Isolde's love, the strength of her spirit, would always resonate through him.

As he walked through the cosmic expanse, he could hear the soft, subtle hum of the stars. Each one held a piece of Isolde's soul, a flickering heartbeat that echoed in the vastness. Her love lived on in every pulse, every burst of light. The stars whispered her name, their energy carrying her essence across the infinite void.

"Isolde…" he said again, his voice more steady now, though his heart still felt fractured. "I will carry your light with me. Always."

But even as he spoke, a shiver of doubt passed through him. Was she truly gone? Could she ever truly be gone? The universe had changed—*he* had changed—but was there still a way for their love to exist beyond the stars? Was there a place for it to live, to grow, even in the silence of her absence?

Lior stopped, his eyes fixed on the brightest cluster of stars in the distance. It was there that he had first felt the spark of their connection, the flicker of her presence that had pulled him toward her. Now, as he looked at the constellation, the light seemed to shimmer in a way that felt different. It felt like… *her.*

Suddenly, the stars above him flickered, their brightness pulsing with an intensity that made his heart race. For a moment, the light seemed to grow brighter, as if something was awakening within the heavens themselves. A soft whisper, like the faintest breath, echoed through the cosmos. It was a voice—so familiar, so full of love, so impossibly distant.

Lior...

His heart skipped a beat, and he took a trembling step forward. "Isolde?"

The voice returned, stronger this time, carrying with it a sense of peace, a quiet, undying presence. *I am here, Lior. Not in the way you remember, but in the light. In the stars.*

Lior's breath caught in his throat. "Isolde, how? How is this possible?"

Our love... it's never truly gone. It's woven into the very fabric of the stars, into the heart of the universe. I am the stars, Lior. And you are part of them, too. You are never alone.

The light from the stars around him swirled and shimmered, their radiance intensifying with each word. He could feel her— feel her presence surrounding him. It was as if she were here, just within reach, her essence flowing through the very air he breathed.

Lior sank to his knees, his heart breaking with the overwhelming flood of emotion that surged through him. "Isolde…" He whispered her name, his voice thick with grief, with joy, with everything he had ever known. "I thought I lost you. I thought you were gone."

I was never truly gone, Isolde's voice responded softly, wrapping around him like a gentle embrace. *I am always with you, Lior. I will never truly leave you.*

The warmth of her words filled him, flooding his soul with peace. The stars seemed to glow brighter, their light pulsing in time with the rhythm of his heartbeat. The love they had shared—though no longer physical—was still alive, still present in the very light that filled the universe. Her soul had become a part of the cosmic order, woven into the very essence of existence.

"I've failed you," Lior murmured, his voice breaking again. "I wasn't able to save you. I couldn't—"

No, Lior, Isolde interrupted, her voice tender and full of reassurance. *You didn't fail me. We both gave everything for the stars. For the universe. You did what needed to be done. You've saved them. And now, my love, you must live. For me. For us.*

The stars around him swirled with a new intensity, their light brighter than it had ever been. It was as if the very cosmos itself had exhaled, filling the void with the essence of Isolde's sacrifice, her love. He could feel it. He could feel her. In the very energy that pulsed through him, in every flicker of starlight, she was there.

And in that moment, Lior understood. Isolde had not truly left him. She was in the stars, in the universe, and in him. She was the heartbeat of the cosmos, her love a force that transcended time and space. It was eternal.

Tears streamed down his face, but they were no longer tears of sorrow. They were tears of peace, of understanding. Isolde was gone in the way he had known her, but she was never gone. She had become part of the very thing they had fought to protect. She was the universe now, and she would never be forgotten.

"I will live, Isolde," he whispered, his voice steady with conviction. "For you. For the stars. For all of it. And I will carry your love with me. Always."

The stars seemed to shine brighter in response, their brilliance a reflection of his promise. He could feel her, still there, a faint pulse of energy in the fabric of the universe. A promise that would echo across time.

The universe, though forever changed by their sacrifice, was now at peace.

And as the stars continued to burn brightly, Lior rose to his feet. He was not alone. Not truly. For in the light of the stars, he would always find her.

Forever, and beyond.

Fourteen

Echoes in the Night Sky

The sky above had changed.

The once bleak expanse of darkness, filled only with scattered and flickering stars, now sprawled across the heavens like a great celestial tapestry. The stars burned brighter, their light more vibrant, their patterns more defined. The cosmos seemed to hum with life, each glowing point in the sky a testament to the rebirth of the universe. But it wasn't just the stars themselves that had changed. It was the very air, the fabric of existence. The universe itself seemed to breathe a little more deeply, as if its pulse had returned to a natural rhythm after years of being out of sync.

Lior stood at the edge of the high tower, the wind whipping around him, the cool night air caressing his face. His gaze was fixed on the heavens above, tracing the constellations that now twinkled in the sky, their light steady and unyielding. He could still feel Isolde's presence there, like an unspoken promise. Her essence—her love—was woven into every gleam of light, every shift of the stars.

She is still with me.

The thought echoed through his mind, the realization that though she was no longer physically by his side, her soul had become one with the universe, like the stars she had loved so dearly. He could feel her in the shimmer of the night sky, in the pulse of starlight. Her love had been woven into the cosmos itself, and with every breath he took, with every flicker of starlight, he knew she was there, living on in the very fabric of the universe.

But the pain of her absence was still there, an ever-present ache that gnawed at the edges of his heart. He had lived through countless lifetimes, had been a protector of the stars for centuries, and yet the depth of their connection had left an indelible mark. He had watched her sacrifice herself for him, for the stars. And in that sacrifice, she had become more than just the woman he loved. She had become the universe's heartbeat.

Yet here he stood, alone, looking up at the stars, knowing that even though the universe had been reborn, there was an emptiness that would never truly be filled.

The wind howled again, and Lior closed his eyes, letting it wash over him. The night sky stretched endlessly before him, filled with stars that seemed to glow brighter than ever before. Each flicker, each shimmer, reminded him of Isolde—the light she had once carried and had given back to the universe.

He remembered the moment of her sacrifice—when she had let go of everything she knew, everything she had been, to give the universe a chance to heal. Her love had been a beacon, a guiding light that had broken the darkness that had threatened to consume everything. And even now, months later, he could still feel her love. It pulsed in the very stars that surrounded him, alive and radiant.

"Isolde," he whispered to the night sky, his voice breaking on the name. The wind carried the sound away, dissipating it into the vastness.

Her name was all that he had left. Her love was all that he had left.

The stars above seemed to respond, their light flickering brighter in his vision. For a moment, he could almost feel her presence next to him, could almost hear the soft melody of her voice, like a memory carried on the wind.

Lior...

The voice—soft, like a whisper of wind on a summer night— stirred something deep within him. His heart caught in his chest as he spun around, his gaze darting to the edge of the tower. But there was no one there. The wind whispered in the empty space, but nothing more. He swallowed hard, his chest tightening as the ache deepened.

He was alone.

But not entirely.

Lior closed his eyes again, reaching out with every sense he had, listening for her, feeling for her. And in the quiet of the night, he could feel it—a faint pulse of energy, a whisper of something beyond the veil of the stars.

She's still with me. She's still here, Lior. Always.

The words echoed in his mind, filling him with a deep sense of peace, a fleeting comfort that he could hold onto, even as the pain of her absence clawed at him. His heart had been shattered when she had faded, but this connection—this bond—had never truly been severed. He could feel her, not as a physical presence, but as a part of the stars themselves. Her love had become one with them.

He stepped away from the tower's edge, turning back toward the heart of the celestial realm—the great temple at the center of the universe where the Heart of the Tower resided, the place where it all began. He could feel the pulse of the stars grow stronger as he neared the temple, their brilliance shifting with every step he took. The sacred space was alive, vibrant, as though the very structure had been reborn with the universe.

As Lior approached the Heart, the air thickened with power. The Heart of the Tower pulsed softly, the ancient energy it contained humming through the air like a living, breathing entity. It was the soul of the universe, the source of all light, of all life. He had come here countless times before, but tonight, it felt different.

The universe, it seemed, was always changing—always shifting. And so was he.

Lior stepped into the center of the temple, the walls gleaming with the glow of starlight. The floor beneath his feet was a map of the stars, constellations and galaxies swirling in patterns that seemed to dance with life. In the center of the room stood the Heart, an immense crystal-like structure that pulsed with energy, a deep blue light radiating from its core.

Lior stood before it, feeling the pull of its energy, the weight of its power. It was here that the universe had been made, here that the celestial order had been forged. And it was here, now, that he would find the answer.

He reached out toward the Heart, his hand trembling as he felt the cosmic energy surge toward him. The power within it was overwhelming, both beautiful and terrifying. The Heart had once been his guide, the source of his strength as a protector of the stars. But now, it seemed like a distant memory—something he could never touch again.

You have been reborn, Lior.

The voice was soft, ethereal, yet powerful. It seemed to come from the very core of the universe itself, and Lior's heart raced as he realized who it was.

Isolde...

Yes, Lior. I am here, in the stars. I am part of them now. But I will always be with you.

Tears filled Lior's eyes as the warmth of her words wrapped around him, filling the empty space where her presence had once been. She was the stars now—woven into the fabric of existence, alive in every flicker, every pulse of light. And yet, even as her form had faded, she was still there. Still connected to him.

I love you, Lior whispered, his voice thick with emotion. *I will always love you.*

And I will always love you, Lior. Don't forget that. We will always be part of each other, no matter where the stars take us.

Lior stood in the center of the temple, the pulse of the Heart surrounding him, feeling her presence filling every corner of the universe. She was still there—alive in the stars. Alive in every whisper of the cosmos.

And he knew, with a certainty that burned brighter than any star, that no matter how much time passed, no matter how far apart they were, their love would continue to echo through the heavens. The universe itself had been shaped by their bond, and now, it would carry them both forward, their love eternal.

Lior closed his eyes, the tears now flowing freely down his face. His heart was heavy, but in the deepest part of his soul, he felt peace. The stars burned brightly, their light never to fade again. And Isolde's love—for him, for the universe—would always burn brighter than any darkness that might threaten to consume them.

As he stood before the Heart, his body trembling with the power of the stars, he could feel the universe begin to hum with a new rhythm—a rhythm that resonated in the deepest part of his being. He had lost her, yes. But she had not truly left. She was the stars now, and he was part of her, as much as she was a part of him.

And together, they would continue to protect the universe, their love forever written in the heavens.

The stars burned brighter than they ever had before.

And in their glow, Lior found a peace that would carry him through eternity.

The Heart pulsed again, a steady beat of life echoing through the vast emptiness of space. Lior remained rooted to the ground, his hand still hovering above the shimmering crystal, feeling its power seep into him, filling the space around him with an energy that was both awe-inspiring and terrifying. The connection between him and Isolde seemed to grow, like an invisible thread that stretched across time and space, threading through the stars themselves. He felt her essence, her love, wrapping around him like a cloak, warming him from within.

Though she was no longer with him in the way he had known her, Lior could still feel her presence. It was in every flicker of light, in every pulse of energy. The stars themselves seemed to hum with the memory of her love. The universe— his universe—was her legacy. And now, her soul was part of it all.

He exhaled slowly, his breath shaky, as he slowly withdrew

his hand from the Heart. He wasn't sure what he had expected to happen, but the power of the Heart had overwhelmed him, flooding him with a sense of deep connection—not just to Isolde, but to the stars, to the very fabric of existence itself. He could feel their energy, their lives, entwined with his own.

"Isolde…" he murmured again, a soft plea against the stillness of the temple. But this time, there was no sorrow in his voice. Only the acceptance of what had been, and what would always be. His love for her would never die. It couldn't. She was the stars now. She had *become* them.

And with that, something inside of him shifted. The ache of her absence, which had gnawed at him for so long, began to fade. He felt a sense of peace wash over him, a quiet acceptance that had eluded him for months. She was not gone. She had not left him. She was part of the universe now, just as he was. And as long as the stars burned, their love would continue to echo through the heavens.

Lior turned away from the Heart, his eyes now scanning the cosmic expanse beyond. The stars, so bright, so steady in their newfound brilliance, seemed to pulse in response to his gaze. It was as if they were alive, each one a living being, a flickering heartbeat of the universe. Their light now felt different—stronger, more enduring. Their energy no longer fluctuated like it had before, wavering between life and death. They were now a symbol of the love that had healed them. A love that had restored balance.

He could feel it, too. His own power, once tainted by loss and grief, now felt steady, grounding him in the reality of this reborn universe. The love he had for Isolde—though it had begun as something fragile and fleeting—had become something eternal, woven into the very fabric of existence. Her spirit, her soul, was a part of everything. In every flicker of starlight, he would find her. She would be with him, always.

As Lior stood there, the sounds of the cosmos, of the universe stretching out in all directions, filled his ears. The wind had shifted, a gentle breeze that carried the scent of something ancient, something eternal. It was the echo of the stars, of the universe itself, alive in the wind.

And then, as if in response to the stillness that hung in the air, something moved—something deep in the heart of the stars. A soft pulse of light, almost imperceptible at first, then growing brighter and more distinct. It spread across the heavens, like a ripple moving outward from the very center of the cosmos. And Lior felt it—felt the change in the energy, the shifting of something ancient, something *alive*. His heart raced as he realized that it was not just the stars that were burning brighter. The entire universe, the very essence of existence, was shifting.

The pulse grew stronger, brighter, until it became a wave—a wave of energy that flowed through the stars, through the galaxies, through the entire celestial realm. Lior's chest tightened as he felt the universe respond, as though it were awakening to something he couldn't fully understand.

And then, in the midst of this wave of cosmic energy, he felt it—her presence. *Isolde.*

The warmth of her love, the spark of her spirit, flooded through him like a surge of light, filling him from the inside out. He staggered back, his breath catching in his throat as the light of the stars grew even brighter. He could feel it now, more strongly than ever—the pulse of her love, her soul, resonating through the universe.

Lior...

Her voice was there again, soft and distant, like a whisper

carried on the wind. But this time, it wasn't just a memory. It wasn't just a fleeting echo. It was her. It was *real*.

I am here, Lior. Always. Not in the way you knew me, but in the stars. I am in every flicker, every burst of light. I am a part of everything now. And so are you.

Lior's knees buckled, and he sank to the ground, his hand reaching out for the starlight that seemed to pour from the heavens. Her voice wrapped around him like the gentlest of caresses, and though he could not see her, he could feel her. The warmth of her presence. The strength of her love. It enveloped him, wrapping him in a light so bright that it made him forget about the darkness, the pain, the loss.

She was the stars. And he was part of them. And together, they were eternal.

Don't mourn me, Isolde's voice whispered in his mind. *I am not lost. I have become what I was always meant to be. And so have you.*

Lior closed his eyes, a single tear slipping down his cheek as he allowed himself to feel the fullness of her love, the immensity of what she had given, and what they had shared. He could feel her all around him—her love, her warmth, her soul—woven into every star, every flicker of light. She was alive in the universe. She was in every breath he took. In every pulse of energy.

He inhaled deeply, grounding himself in the cosmic rhythm, in the steady pulse of the universe. The stars, now more brilliant than ever before, burned brightly above him, and their light seemed to shine with the strength of their shared love.

He felt it then—the bond between them, strong and unbroken, stretching across the universe, beyond time and space.

The universe, in all its vastness, was a reflection of their love. And though they were separated by realms beyond comprehension, Lior knew that they would never truly be apart.

Isolde had not left him. She had become part of the universe itself. And in that knowledge, Lior found peace.

He stood slowly, his gaze fixed on the heavens above him, the stars shining brighter than ever before. His heart swelled with the love they had shared, the love that had saved the universe. He could feel Isolde, feel her love, alive in every star, in every flicker of light. And as long as the stars burned, so too would their love.

The universe had been reborn.

And so, their love would continue to echo through the heavens, forever.

The night sky stretched out before him, vast and eternal, but no longer empty. The stars—brighter, steadier, more alive than they had ever been—shone down upon him, a testament to the bond that had saved them all.

And as Lior gazed up at the heavens, the stars burned brighter than they ever had before.

And he knew, with every beat of his heart, that Isolde's love would never fade. It would live on in the stars. Forever.

Fifteen

The Warden's Legacy

The wind howled through the endless expanse of the celestial realm, carrying with it the whispers of a thousand lost dreams and fading memories. It stirred the scattered remnants of the old world—fragments of light, echoes of energy that had once defined the universe. The air was thick with the energy of transformation, as the very fabric of the cosmos shifted and breathed with new life.

Isolde's sacrifice, her love, had done more than restore the balance—it had rewritten the laws of the stars. The universe was no longer what it had once been. It had grown, evolved, and been reshaped by the sacrifices of those who had fought to protect it. Isolde and Lior's bond had become a force of its own, an unbreakable thread that wove through the stars and the hearts of all those who had come before and after. But even as the cosmos breathed a new rhythm, there was a lingering heaviness in the air.

The wardens, the ancient protectors who had once stood as guardians of the stars, now gathered at the precipice of a new era. Their duty had shifted. No longer were they merely protectors—they were part of something greater, something alive and growing, something that would shape the future of the universe. And yet, in the quiet between the stars, their hearts were heavy with the loss of the one who had led them all, the one who had shown them what love truly was.

Isolde.

Her memory lingered in the very stars themselves, her sacrifice, her love, still alive in the energy of the universe. But as the wardens stood before the vast expanse of the cosmic plane, they knew that their work was not done. The universe had been saved, but the work of ensuring its continued balance had only just begun.

The stars, once cold and distant, now pulsed with life, a new energy flowing through them. They were no longer just celestial bodies; they were living beings with destinies of their own. Just as Isolde and Lior had once been bound by love, so too were the stars now bound to one another, their fates intertwined in ways the wardens had never imagined.

The celestial council had convened in the heart of the ancient tower, a vast, spiraling spire of light and stone that reached from the depths of the universe to the very edge of reality. Inside, the wardens gathered, their forms cloaked in shimmering light, their faces hidden beneath the ancient hoods of their sacred order. They were no longer the same as they had been before. The sacrifice of Isolde and the love she had shared with Lior had changed them all, and now, they stood at the threshold of a new destiny.

High above the council hall, the Heart of the Tower pulsed

with a steady rhythm, its light flickering in time with the heartbeat of the universe itself. It was here that the first warden had made the ultimate sacrifice long ago, and it was here that the final decision would be made.

One of the wardens, a tall figure cloaked in deep blue, stepped forward. His presence, though silent, commanded attention. His eyes—hidden beneath his hood—glowed faintly with the energy of the stars. He was the leader now, the one who had taken the mantle from Isolde in her final moments, the one who had vowed to carry on her legacy. His name was Eryx, and his heart, like that of all the wardens, carried the weight of a universe reborn.

"We stand at the crossroads of destiny," Eryx said, his voice low and steady, filled with the weight of centuries. "The stars are no longer mere lights in the sky. They are living, breathing entities—each with its own soul, its own path. But with this gift comes a curse. We are no longer the guardians of the stars. We are their stewards. We must ensure that they remain in balance, that they do not falter as they did before. The love that saved them must now guide us. But we are not alone in this. The darkness still lingers, waiting for its moment."

A murmur passed through the gathered wardens, a ripple of unease. Though the stars had been reborn, their stability was not guaranteed. The balance between light and dark, fire and water, was delicate, and it would take more than the sacrifice of a single soul to ensure that the universe remained intact.

Eryx continued, his eyes lifting to the great expanse of stars visible through the towering windows of the council hall. "We must learn to listen to the stars, to understand their needs. They are more than mere guardians; they are the heartbeat of this universe. And just as Isolde and Lior's love has become part of them, so too must we become part of the stars. We will not be mere protectors anymore. We will be their guides. And in return, they will guide us."

There was silence in the room. The wardens—once detached from the universe they protected—now felt its pulse within them. They were not the same as they had been before. They had seen the light and the darkness, had lived through the sacrifices of the past, and now they had to carry that knowledge forward, carrying the weight of the love that had birthed this new reality.

From the farthest corner of the hall, a figure stepped forward, his presence felt more than seen. He was a younger warden, a new addition to the council, though his gaze was steady and full of the wisdom of someone who had witnessed the depths of the universe's struggles. His name was Kael, and though he was new to the order, he had come to understand the importance of the stars in a way that few others had. His voice, when he spoke, was filled with the weight of this newfound responsibility.

"What of the darkness?" Kael asked, his voice cutting through the silence like a blade. "Tharion's fall has not eradicated all the shadows that lurk. The imbalance that remains in the cosmos, the forces of fire and water—can we truly maintain that balance without confronting them directly?"

Eryx nodded solemnly. "The darkness is never truly gone. It is woven into the very fabric of the universe, just as light is. And there are forces at work, forces that are waiting for an opening, a weakness. But we have something now that we didn't before. We have each other. And we have the stars."

"The stars are alive now," another warden, a woman named Lyra, added. Her eyes gleamed as she spoke, the light of the stars reflected in her gaze. "They were never meant to be controlled, only guarded. But now, we must learn to listen. We must learn from them. Their destinies are now intertwined with our own."

The room fell into a tense silence as the wardens exchanged glances, the weight of their responsibilities pressing down on them. The stars were no longer distant and cold; they were alive, breathing, their paths now intertwined with the lives of those who had once guarded them. But as Lyra had said, their destinies were now theirs to shape. The universe, it seemed, had given them the power to direct the course of the stars. And in that power lay great responsibility.

"We must begin with the oldest of the stars," Eryx said, his voice resolute. "The first star, the one who led us all, the one who showed us what love could do. We begin with Isolde. Her legacy, her love, will guide us as we move forward. But we must learn to move beyond the mistakes of the past. We must learn to accept the stars as living beings, not mere symbols."

The council nodded, the weight of Eryx's words sinking in. The room was filled with the quiet hum of the stars, the soft whispers of their energy brushing against the walls of the tower. Their light flickered, more steady now than ever before, as though they were waiting, listening, for the wardens to act.

Eryx raised his hand, and the room fell silent. "The time has come to forge a new path. The path of the stars and the warden will no longer be one of separation. We are bound to them now, just as they are bound to us. Our duty is no longer to simply guard them. It is to understand them. To guide them. And, if necessary, to fight for them."

There was a tension in the air, palpable and heavy, but beneath it, there was a quiet hope. The wardens had always been silent sentinels, standing apart from the universe they protected. But now, they would step forward. They would become a part of the very fabric of existence.

Eryx's eyes scanned the room one last time, and for the first time since the death of Isolde, he felt something stir within him—something that had been missing for far too long. A sense of purpose. A sense of unity.

"The legacy of the warden and the star lives on," he said softly, his voice full of reverence. "We will carry it forward, with love and honor. Together."

And as the final words echoed through the hall, the stars outside burned brighter, their light flickering in response to the power of the wardens' commitment. The cosmos was changing, shifting, evolving. And the wardens, with the guidance of the stars and the legacy of love that had birthed them, would shape the future of the universe.

The dawn of a new era had begun.

The room was still, each warden standing in solemn contemplation, the weight of Eryx's words hanging in the air like an unspoken oath. The stars outside twinkled steadily, their light glowing brighter and sharper than ever before, as though reflecting the hope and uncertainty that now pulsed through the hearts of the wardens.

Eryx lowered his hand, and for the first time, he allowed himself to feel the immense power that had settled within the council. The stars were not just celestial bodies now; they were living, breathing entities, and their destinies, like the wardens', were bound to each other in ways that neither side had fully understood before. The universe had grown larger, more complex, more delicate. The stakes were higher than they had ever been, and now it was up to the wardens to guide the stars and protect them, not from darkness alone, but from the forces of their own creation.

"We must go to the First Constellation," Eryx announced, his voice calm but filled with quiet authority. "The one Isolde and Lior loved most. It is there that the next chapter of the stars begins."

A murmur rippled through the council as the wardens began to stir, the silence that had once consumed them now filled with a sense of purpose. The First Constellation—glowing brilliantly in the distance, once a symbol of hope and now, a reminder of the love that had shaped their fates. Its light was a beacon, both to those who had lived and loved under it, and to the new generation of wardens who had come to carry its legacy forward.

"We cannot wait any longer," Lyra said, her voice filled with determination. "The stars are still unstable. We have seen how easily they can falter. How easily they can be consumed by the darkness. If we do not act now, we may lose everything."

Eryx nodded. "I agree. The stars have been reborn, yes. But they have not been fully restored. The balance we fought for must be maintained. The energies of the stars have been stretched, torn, by the darkness, and now it is our task to ensure that the equilibrium is not upset again."

A figure moved forward from the back of the room—a shadow among shadows. It was Kael, the youngest of the wardens, but one who had always demonstrated a surprising depth of insight. His eyes were wide, filled with the intensity of someone who had witnessed the raw, chaotic force of the stars' struggles.

"What if it's already too late?" Kael's voice cut through the growing tension. "The stars may be alive now, but their fates are still in flux. How can we be sure that we can maintain their stability? What if the darkness was not just Tharion's, but something more insidious? Something that lurks beyond our understanding?"

His words hung in the air, and Eryx felt a tightness in his chest. The question was not one he had avoided, but the answer was something far more complex than anyone could truly grasp. He had seen the stars burn and flicker, consumed by shadows, and he had watched as Isolde and Lior had sacrificed everything to restore them. But even now, there was a lingering fear—a fear that the darkness would rise again, more powerful, more insidious than before.

"We have no choice but to try," Eryx replied, his tone resolute. "We cannot afford to lose more. Not after everything we've sacrificed. We must go to the First Constellation. If we are to guide the stars, we must first understand them. And that means facing the darkness head-on."

His gaze swept over the wardens—each one standing at the edge of destiny, bound by duty, by the love that had forged them, and by the knowledge that their actions would echo throughout the universe. The fate of the stars, of the celestial realms, lay in their hands.

A deep silence followed, broken only by the distant hum of the universe itself—the soft, steady pulse of the stars' energy. Their light flickered, almost as if they were waiting for the wardens to act, to rise to the occasion and embrace the legacy that had been handed down to them.

"Let us go," Eryx said at last, his voice filled with quiet authority. "The stars need us."

With that, the council filed out of the hall, their cloaks flowing behind them as they made their way toward the great chamber where the portals to the celestial realms awaited them. The air seemed to vibrate with the energy of the stars, each warden walking in silent reverence, the gravity of the moment hanging heavy around them.

Lior's absence was still a raw ache in his heart. Eryx could feel it—he could feel it in the very air, in the vibrations of the universe, in the subtle pulse of the stars. Isolde and Lior had shaped the universe in their love. And now, the wardens were the stewards of that legacy, tasked with ensuring that the stars continued to burn brightly, that they never flickered out again.

The portal opened before them, the massive, swirling vortex of energy that connected them to the First Constellation. Eryx stepped forward, leading the wardens into the swirling currents of light, the stars above them twinkling in greeting. The air around them hummed with power, and Eryx could feel the call of the stars—a beckoning, a pull to go forward, to understand, to restore.

As the wardens passed through the portal, they emerged into the heart of the First Constellation. It was a place of infinite beauty—glistening stars clustered together in intricate patterns, their light flowing in brilliant streams of energy that seemed to pulse with a life of their own. The entire constellation was alive, vibrant, and humming with cosmic energy.

At the center of the First Constellation stood a towering spire of crystal, its surface glimmering with the light of a thousand stars. It was the source of the First Constellation's power, the heart of the universe, where light and dark were held in perfect balance. But it was not invulnerable. Eryx could feel the disturbance in the air—the ripple of instability that still lingered, like a shadow threatening to swallow the stars.

"Isolde…" Lyra whispered as she gazed upon the heart of the constellation, her voice thick with emotion. "This is where she gave herself. This is where she became part of the stars."

Eryx closed his eyes for a moment, the weight of those words settling over him. The sacrifice. The love. The bond that had been formed between Isolde, Lior, and the stars had altered the very course of the universe. But that bond was fragile, as fragile as the stars themselves. And now, it was their responsibility to ensure that the balance they had fought for remained intact.

"We are here for Isolde," Eryx said, his voice steady, though his heart ached with the memory of her. "We are here to carry on her legacy. To protect what she loved."

The wardens stood in a circle around the spire, their hands raised as they called upon the power of the stars. Light poured from the constellation, flowing into their bodies, filling them with a deep, steadying energy. Eryx could feel the power of the stars flooding through him, grounding him in the present moment, but also connecting him to the past—Isolde's past. Her sacrifice was not in vain. They would not let it be.

The heart of the First Constellation pulsed brightly, its light growing stronger with each passing second. But with that light came a new understanding—a realization that the work was far from over. The darkness still lingered, waiting for its chance to strike.

Eryx reached out, his fingers brushing against the cool surface of the crystal. The stars above them flickered in response, their light bending toward him, as if they were listening. He could feel the weight of their gaze—their hope, their expectation.

"We will honor you, Isolde," Eryx whispered, his voice firm with the weight of his promise. "We will carry your love

forward, through the stars, through time itself."
The stars shone brighter than ever before.
And the legacy of the warden and the star lived on.

Sixteen

Whispers of the Heart

The wind rustled through the trees, carrying with it the distant murmur of the cosmos, a soft hum that seemed to vibrate through Lior's very soul. He stood at the edge of the cliff, the ground beneath him solid but the air above uncertain, as though the universe itself was in a constant state of flux. The stars above him gleamed brightly in the ink-black sky, their brilliance casting long shadows across the land. The moon, pale and ethereal, hung in the heavens, bathing the world below in silver light, and Lior's heart—so full of love, loss, and longing—ached in time with the steady rhythm of the universe.

It had been months since Isolde had given her life for the stars. Since she had become one with the very essence of the cosmos. And still, her absence felt as raw and as fresh as the day she had faded into the starlight.

But she was not gone.

The bond between them, forged in the fires of sacrifice and bound by the love they shared, was unbroken. Lior could feel her in everything—the soft glow of the stars, the whispers of the wind, the pulse of the earth beneath his feet. Though she no longer walked beside him, her presence was as undeniable as the light of the moon.

He closed his eyes, breathing in the cool night air, and felt her voice whisper through the breeze. It was faint, like the flutter of a moth's wings, but it was unmistakable. Isolde's voice.

Lior...

He could hear it as clearly as though she were standing beside him, her voice carried on the wind, weaving through the tendrils of the night. His chest tightened, the ache of her absence stirring in him again.

I am with you, always.

Lior's eyes fluttered open, his gaze lifting to the heavens above. The stars blinked down at him, their soft glow brighter now than ever before, and he felt the warmth of Isolde's spirit wrapping around him like a familiar embrace. He reached out with his hand, his fingers trembling, not in fear, but in the deep, unyielding love that he carried for her, even in her absence.

"I love you," he whispered into the night, his voice hoarse, thick with the weight of everything he had lost and everything he had gained. "I will love you forever, Isolde. Forever."

The stars seemed to shimmer in response, the light pulsing around him, as though they, too, were listening to the depths of his soul. Lior had spent countless nights like this, standing at the edge of the world, talking to her, whispering his love into the universe. In the quiet moments between day and night, when the world held its breath, he could feel her presence—her essence—still with him. Their bond was not bound by space, not limited by time or the boundaries of the physical realm. Their love had transcended all that.

But even as he spoke her name, the weight of loneliness pressed down on him. There were no more shared smiles between them, no more soft touches, no more whispered secrets in the dark. His world felt… empty without her, as if something irreplaceable had been torn from his soul.

Lior's chest ached, the sharp sting of loss still fresh despite the months that had passed. The stars above burned brightly, their light steady, but even they could not fill the hollow space left by Isolde's absence.

But then, as though the universe itself were answering his grief, the wind shifted, carrying with it a faint scent, like the softest touch of the ocean breeze. It was warm and familiar, and for a moment, Lior's breath caught in his throat. He could feel it—a presence, a flicker of warmth. And then, like a whisper in the silence of his mind, the words came, soft and gentle:

I am here.

He closed his eyes again, and this time, when he breathed in, he could almost feel her beside him, as though the air itself had transformed into her presence. Isolde was not gone. She was a part of the stars, of the universe, and through their bond, she would always be with him.

A strange calmness washed over Lior, the tightness in his chest easing slightly. He stood there, bathed in moonlight, the night stretching out around him like an endless ocean, and he could almost feel her smile. He could almost hear her laugh. The warmth of her love was still there, woven into every flicker of light, every shift of the air, every whisper of the stars.

We will be reunited, Lior.

The words were clear now, louder in his mind, as if she were standing beside him, whispering in his ear. His heart swelled with the fullness of it. She had not abandoned him. She was not lost. She was the stars. She was the light that had healed the universe, and she was the love that still echoed through his every heartbeat.

"I will wait for you," Lior murmured into the wind, his voice filled with both sorrow and joy. "I will wait for as long as it takes. Until the day we are together again."

The stars seemed to pulse in response, their light growing brighter with each word he spoke. Lior felt the universe respond to his vow, the very air around him humming with the energy of the cosmos. His bond with Isolde had not been severed; it had been transformed, made eternal by her sacrifice and his love. And though they were no longer together in the physical realm, they would always be intertwined. The stars, with their steady, eternal glow, would be the testament to their love, a love that transcended all boundaries.

Lior stepped forward, feeling the cool earth beneath his feet as he walked toward the edge of the cliff. He stood at the precipice, the wind tugging at his cloak, the vastness of the universe stretching out before him. The night was alive, the stars burning bright in the sky, the moon hanging high above him like a silent sentinel.

And in that silence, in the quiet of the night, he could hear her again.

Lior...

Her voice, soft and filled with love, drifted through the air, and Lior smiled to himself, his heart filling with warmth.

"I'm here," he whispered, his voice carrying into the night. "I will always be here. Watching the stars. Watching for you."

The stars twinkled in response, their brilliance unwavering, their light constant and true. And as Lior stood there, on the edge of the world, he knew in his heart that Isolde was with him, forever part of the stars, and that one day, their love would shine together once more.

For now, all he could do was wait. And love her in the way the stars loved the universe—steadfast, eternal, and undying.

The night continued its quiet rhythm, the world turning, the universe moving ever onward. But in Lior's heart, time had stopped, and the stars had never been brighter.

Lior stood at the edge of the cliff, the wind caressing his face like the tender touch of Isolde's hand, and yet, the emptiness of her absence felt more profound than it ever had before. His heart, once filled with the intensity of their shared love, now ached with a quiet ache, a reminder that though the universe had been saved, the cost had been more than just the loss of a life—it had been the loss of the one person who had truly seen him, loved him, and made him whole.

The wind swept through the vastness, bringing with it the sound of the stars, their voices a soft, celestial hum. They were alive, those stars, their light more vibrant than ever, their energy coursing through the very fabric of the universe. But tonight, as Lior stood alone, their glow felt distant, a light that shone for others, yet felt unreachable to him.

As if the universe itself could sense his loneliness, a subtle shift in the air tugged at him. The stars twinkled, their light shimmering like distant memories. And with it, a presence swept into his soul.

Lior...

Her voice—soft, familiar, eternal—drifted like a whisper through the expanse. It was faint at first, barely perceptible, but it made his heart clench, as though she were standing right next to him, just out of reach. Lior's breath caught in his throat, and the world seemed to blur for a moment.

"Isolde?" His voice was barely a breath, carried away by the wind. Was it really her? Could it be?

I am here, came the whisper again, clearer this time, ringing in his mind. *I never left, Lior. I am part of the stars, part of the light. Our love... it has become eternal.*

His heart raced, the ache of grief mingling with a rush of joy. The air around him vibrated, filled with energy, as though the very stars were pulsing in time with the beat of his heart.

"I can feel you," Lior whispered, stepping forward, his gaze fixed on the vast sky above. His eyes searched for the flickering lights of the stars, but he knew now that the connection between them was beyond the physical. "You're in the stars. You're the stars, Isolde."

Yes, she replied softly. *And you are part of me, as I am part of you. Nothing can sever the bond we share, Lior. Not even time, not even space. Our love has become one with the universe.*

Lior's hand reached out toward the heavens, fingers trembling. He could feel the faintest pulse of warmth—a gentle touch against the cold of the night. He felt it in the stars themselves, their light more steady now, more constant, like the steady beat of a heart that could never stop.

"You're here," he said, his voice breaking. "I thought I lost you. I thought the universe had taken you from me."

I will always be here, Lior. With every flicker of light, every beat of the stars' heart, I am with you. The universe is our legacy. Our love has woven into it, like threads that will never break. As long as the stars burn, we will never be apart.

Tears filled Lior's eyes, a raw and painful ache flooding his chest. It wasn't the same as having her beside him, not the way it had been when they shared the same sky, the same breath. But this—this was a different kind of love. A love that had transcended the boundaries of time and space. She was the stars. And in that, they were together, forever.

"I will wait for you," Lior murmured, his voice thick with emotion. "No matter how long it takes. No matter where the stars take us, I will wait for the day when we are reunited."

And I will wait for you, Lior, came Isolde's voice, gentle and full of love. *Even in the deepest corners of the universe, my soul will always find you. Always.*

The stars shimmered brightly in the sky, and in that moment, Lior felt something he hadn't felt in months—peace. It wasn't the absence of pain, but the acceptance of it. The love they had shared, the bond they had formed, had become something greater than either of them could have imagined. Their love had become the very fabric of the universe, woven into every flicker of light. And as long as the stars burned, their love would continue to shine.

Lior closed his eyes, letting the wind brush against his skin, his hair lifting softly as if the universe itself was embracing him. The quiet hum of the stars, the steady pulse of light, filled him with a sense of serenity he hadn't felt in so long. The universe was alive. And Isolde was with him, always.

And then, as if to further confirm her presence, a warm gust of wind swept through the trees, rustling the leaves in the distance. The sound was familiar, like the rustle of Isolde's cloak, like the soft, soothing sound of her laughter echoing through the cosmos. Lior's heart swelled, and for a moment, he thought he could almost see her—her radiant face, her eyes filled with the love they had shared.

But when he opened his eyes, the wind had quieted, and the night was still again, the stars burning brightly above. He could no longer see her, but he could still feel her, so strongly that it was as though she had never truly left.

"I love you, Isolde," Lior whispered into the night once more, his voice carrying on the wind, an offering to the stars. "Forever and always."

And I will love you, Lior. Forever. Her voice, fading now, seemed to wrap around him, filling his heart, his mind. *We are one with the stars. And so, we are eternal.*

The stars above burned brighter, their light reflecting off Lior's tear-soaked face as he gazed up at them, the heavens alive with the love they had shared. The light of the stars seemed to respond to his words, their pulse steady and strong. Isolde's essence was in every one of them, and in that thought, Lior found peace.

The universe was vast, infinite. Yet, in this moment, standing beneath the night sky, Lior knew that no distance, no time, could ever break the bond they had shared. Though the physical world separated them, they were together, forever intertwined in the very heart of the stars.

And as the wind carried her voice away into the vastness of the night, Lior felt a deep sense of gratitude. For the love they had known. For the sacrifice that had saved the universe. For the eternal connection they now shared.

The universe would go on, the stars would burn brightly, and their love would continue to echo in every flicker of light, forever.

Lior took a deep breath, steadying himself as he slowly

turned from the cliff's edge. The stars, so bright above him, seemed to grow even brighter, their light shimmering across the landscape. His heart was full—full of love, full of longing, full of the knowledge that though Isolde was no longer by his side in the way he had known her, she was never truly gone.

She was the stars. And he was a part of her, as she was a part of him.

And that was enough.

With that thought, Lior walked away from the edge, his heart light, his steps sure. He was no longer searching for her. For he knew that wherever he went, she would always be with him.

In the stars. Forever.

Seventeen

The New Dawn

⁓◦⦾◦⁓

The first hint of dawn touched the horizon, painting the sky with hues of crimson and gold. The stars, still burning brightly in the heavens, seemed to pulse in response, their light steady and eternal. Yet, for Lior, the darkness that had once seemed infinite felt closer now. He stood at the edge of the world, the morning light spilling around him, yet his gaze was fixed on the stars, the same stars that had been his solace, his strength, and his connection to Isolde. Her presence lingered in the soft wind that tugged at his cloak, in the steady rhythm of the universe's heartbeat. She was there, somewhere between the stars, woven into the very fabric of the cosmos.

For months, the stars had burned brighter than ever, their light now stronger, more constant. But with each passing day, Lior felt the weight of his new role pressing down on him. He was no longer just a protector of the stars. He was their guardian, a warden in the truest sense of the word. And with that responsibility came an overwhelming sense of duty—a duty that could not be ignored, not when the very balance of the universe hung in the balance.

The wind stirred again, a soft whisper through the trees, and Lior closed his eyes for a moment, as if listening. He could hear her voice in the back of his mind, soft but clear.

You are not alone, Lior. You will never be alone.

Her voice. It had become a constant presence in his mind, a whisper on the wind, a pulse of energy he could feel in the very stars that surrounded him. She had become one with the universe, with the stars that flickered in the heavens. Her sacrifice had ensured that balance had been restored, but her essence, her spirit, lived on in the light of the cosmos. Every flicker of a distant star was a reminder of her love. Every new dawn, a testament to the bond they had shared.

The light of the morning grew stronger, the sky shifting from darkness to dawn in the blink of an eye. Lior stood there, unmoving, lost in his thoughts, his gaze fixed on the vast expanse of the universe above. The stars, now scattered across the sky, were no longer cold, indifferent specks of light. They were alive, each one a living being, with its own soul, its own story to tell. And as their guardian, it was Lior's duty to protect them, to ensure their light would never fade, just as he had promised Isolde.

His heart swelled with a mixture of pride and sorrow. The universe had been saved, yes. But it had come at the cost of something irreplaceable—his love, his soul's counterpart. Isolde was gone from the world, but her legacy remained.

A quiet rumble broke the stillness of the moment, and Lior turned toward it. Far in the distance, the edges of the mountains cast dark shadows across the land, but it was not the land that had drawn his attention—it was the faint disturbance in the air, the soft tremor that he could feel vibrating in his very bones.

Lior narrowed his eyes, stepping closer to the edge of the cliff. Something was wrong. The stillness of the universe that had settled over him was beginning to fracture, the pulse of the stars flickering with something… darker. A sense of unease began to settle in the pit of his stomach. The forces of darkness that had once threatened the stars were not gone—they were merely waiting, biding their time.

He could feel it in the stars. The balance was fragile, still vulnerable to forces beyond his understanding.

Isolde… he thought, his heart heavy with the weight of his emotions. *Give me strength.*

The wind howled again, swirling around him with greater intensity. The air thickened with energy, and for a moment, Lior felt as though the stars themselves were speaking to him, their voices a soft chorus in the back of his mind.

Do not fear, Lior. You are the guardian now. We are with you.

He exhaled slowly, the words of the stars settling over him, filling him with purpose. The light of the dawn shone brighter now, casting long shadows across the land, and Lior stood tall, his resolve hardening like steel.

He had been entrusted with the stars. They had become his responsibility, and with that responsibility came a duty to protect them from the darkness that still lingered on the edges of the universe. He could not allow the sacrifice of Isolde to have been in vain.

The universe had been reborn, and with it came a new era. But the war between light and dark, between fire and water, between life and death, was far from over.

Lior turned away from the cliff's edge and began to walk through the landscape, the path before him lit by the soft glow of the stars. He had been given a second chance, and he would honor it. He would be the guardian the stars needed, the protector they deserved.

The landscape around him seemed to shift and change with each step, as if the land itself was alive, responding to his presence. The trees swayed gently in the wind, the leaves rustling like whispers of secrets long buried. The air was thick with the scent of earth and the promise of something new, something awakening.

But as he walked, his mind wandered again to Isolde. To the love they had shared. The bond that had transcended time, space, and even death itself. He could still feel her, every pulse of energy from the stars reminding him of the sacrifice she had made. Her love had been the force that had saved the universe, and now, even in her absence, that love was the strength that carried him forward.

As the first light of dawn reached its peak, Lior paused. He gazed up at the sky, watching as the stars began to fade, replaced by the pale light of the sun. But even as the stars retreated into the morning light, Lior knew they were never truly gone. They would always be there, their light forever intertwined with his own.

"Isolde," Lior whispered, his voice trembling. "I will continue our journey. For you. For the stars. For us."

And as the dawn spread across the land, its light piercing the darkness, Lior felt a flicker of warmth in his chest. The love they had shared, the bond that had been forged in the stars, would never fade. It would continue to burn bright, even as the world around him shifted, even as the forces of darkness waited in the distance.

The journey was far from over, but Lior was ready. He was the guardian of the stars, and with Isolde's love guiding him, he would never falter.

The universe had been saved. The dawn had broken.

And with it, a new era began.

Lior stood tall, feeling the weight of the stars, feeling the pull of his responsibility, but he also felt the presence of Isolde, her love as constant as the stars above him.

Their story would continue. The stars would burn brighter than ever before.

And he would stand beside them, forever.

Lior stood motionless, gazing up at the horizon as the sun fully emerged, casting its golden light across the vast expanse of the world. The stars had retreated into the background, their soft glow dimming beneath the overpowering light of the new day. Yet, despite the sun's brilliance, Lior could feel them—*the stars*—still burning bright in the fabric of the universe, their light pulsing in time with the beat of his heart.

He was a guardian now. No longer a passive observer, no longer just a protector of the stars' glow. He had become their caretaker, their lifeblood, charged with preserving their existence against the creeping darkness that still threatened from beyond the edges of the universe. But this new reality, this responsibility, weighed heavily on him. His hands had been stained by the cost of their survival, and the absence of Isolde—the sacrifice she had made—lingered in every corner of his being.

Her essence, he could still feel it, like a whisper in the wind.

Her love had once anchored him, guided him through the darkest of times. Now, that love was a beacon—an unbreakable connection to the stars, to the balance she had saved with her sacrifice. It was in every flicker of starlight, in every pulse of cosmic energy that rippled through the fabric of the universe. She was part of it, just as he was, woven together in the great tapestry of existence.

The sound of the wind rustling the leaves of the trees stirred him from his thoughts. Lior closed his eyes, letting the wind wash over him, as if it were carrying messages from Isolde herself. He could almost hear her, faintly, like the breath of a memory he was clinging to with the last vestiges of his strength.

You're never truly alone, Lior. I will always be with you, in the stars, in the light, in the very air you breathe.

The words were like a balm, soothing the ache in his heart, but they could not erase the emptiness of her absence. Her voice was an echo, a shadow, always there yet always just out of reach. A subtle warmth filled his chest, but it wasn't enough. It could never be enough.

Lior's fingers clenched into fists as he turned toward the horizon, his gaze fixed on the distant mountains. He could feel the pull of something else—something dark, something more insidious—lurking at the edges of his consciousness. The forces that had once been quelled by Isolde's sacrifice had not disappeared; they had merely retreated, biding their time.

The stars had been restored, yes. But the war between light and darkness was far from over. The universe was still fragile, still vulnerable. And now, it was up to him to protect it, to honor Isolde's memory by ensuring the balance remained intact.

With a sharp breath, Lior turned away from the edge of the

cliff and began to walk. His footsteps were steady, the weight of his new role settling in with each step. The land around him was alive—alive in a way he hadn't fully realized until now. The wind carried the scent of fresh earth, of life and growth, as though the universe itself was breathing in time with him.

He walked for hours, across fields where the first signs of spring were just beginning to show—the buds of new flowers pushing through the soil, the grass swaying in the gentle breeze. The world was waking up, growing, shifting. Just like the stars, it was alive.

But the quiet beauty of the landscape was marred by an unsettling sense of urgency, a constant reminder that time was running out. The darkness was not gone. It never truly would be.

He had to be vigilant.

The sound of the wind grew louder, more insistent, and as Lior walked deeper into the forest that bordered the cliffs, the air seemed to change. It was cooler now, heavier, laden with the weight of something unknown. The very trees around him seemed to lean closer, as though the land itself was warning him. His instincts flared, and he stopped dead in his tracks, the hairs on the back of his neck rising.

He felt it then, a presence in the air, a weight that pressed against his chest. The stars, for the first time in months, flickered unnervingly, their steady glow wavering like a candle flame buffeted by the wind. His heart raced as he stepped forward, scanning the surroundings.

The forest was still, almost eerily so. The usual rustling of leaves, the sound of animals moving through the underbrush, was absent. It was as though the world had gone quiet in anticipation of something terrible.

A shadow moved at the edge of his vision.

Lior's eyes darted to the source, his body tensing as he readied himself for whatever danger might emerge. The shadow flickered again, this time more distinct, more deliberate. And then, in the soft light of the fading sun, a figure stepped forward.

A man. Tall, cloaked in darkness, with eyes glowing like embers. His presence was cold, unnatural, and as he emerged from the shadows, the stars above seemed to dim in response, as if they, too, recognized the threat.

"Lior, guardian of the stars," the man's voice was low, smooth, and filled with a mocking tone. "How interesting to find you here, all alone. The stars have not forgotten you. But neither have the shadows."

Lior's heart skipped a beat. His hand instinctively went to the hilt of the sword at his side, his fingers tightening around the cool metal. This figure—this presence—was no stranger. The man before him was one of the ancient darknesses that had once roamed freely, feeding on the light, consuming the very essence of the stars. But now, something had changed. The man was no longer just a shadow; he was something more. Something ancient.

"Who are you?" Lior demanded, his voice steady but filled with the tension that coiled in his chest. The stars, the steady pulse of light he had felt for so long, were flickering—warring against the presence of this figure.

The man smiled, the expression twisted, cruel. "You do not remember me, do you? I have been watching you, Lior. Watching your every step, waiting for the right moment to strike."

Lior's heart thundered in his chest. His mind raced. He had

seen this figure before, somewhere deep in his memories—before the sacrifice of Isolde, before the rebirth of the stars. This darkness had once been a force of chaos, a herald of destruction. And yet, now, it was something more.

"What do you want?" Lior asked, his grip tightening on his sword.

The man's eyes glinted with an eerie light. "The balance has been restored, yes. But balance does not last. Nothing lasts forever, especially not light. You, Lior, are the guardian of the stars. But there is one thing you have forgotten." His smile widened. "The stars can be extinguished, just as they were once born."

Lior's breath caught in his throat. The man's words echoed in the silence, sending a chill through him. He knew what this meant. The universe might have been restored, but it could still fall. The stars—their very essence—could still be consumed, just as easily as it had been before.

The man raised his hand, and the darkness around him seemed to swirl like smoke, coalescing into a form, a shape that was almost human but not quite. It was something darker, something older. Lior stepped back, his heart pounding, as the man took another step forward, the very air crackling with energy.

The stars above flickered again, their light dimming as the dark figure advanced. He had not come alone. The shadows, long dormant, were awakening once more.

Lior's pulse quickened. His gaze shifted to the distance, where the stars were flickering more violently now, like they, too, could sense the danger that approached. He could feel the pull of the darkness—the growing, insidious weight that threatened to swallow the very light he had fought to protect.

And he knew, in that moment, that this was only the beginning.

The darkness had returned.

And it was stronger than before.

The stars were no longer just a beacon of light. They were a battlefield.

And Lior would fight for them, for Isolde's legacy, and for the balance that could slip away in an instant.

With a deep breath, he drew his sword, the gleaming steel catching the light of the stars above. His grip tightened, his resolve hardening. The fight for the stars had just begun, and this time, it would not be so easily won.

The man's smile widened, but it wasn't one of victory. It was one of understanding.

"This time, Lior," he whispered, "you will see that darkness is not just a force you can fight. It is the one thing that can never be extinguished."

And with those words, the battle began.

Eighteen

The End of Eternity

The universe was vast—far too vast to be fully understood. Even after everything Lior had seen, everything he had endured, there were still depths of the cosmos that remained a mystery. The stars that once seemed so far away now felt intimately close, their light flickering in time with his own heartbeat. Each night, as he stood beneath the endless sky, he felt himself more connected to the universe than ever before. He could feel the pulse of the stars in his veins, could sense the life and death of the stars like the rhythm of his own breath.

The weight of the cosmos was both his burden and his gift, and now, as the guardian of the stars, it was a responsibility that Lior bore alone.

Each day bled into the next—each night felt like an eternity. He wandered the celestial plains, his mind fixed on his duties, though his heart always drifted to the same place: the stars.

The stars, and Isolde. Her absence had become a constant presence in his life, as real and as tangible as the light that poured from the heavens. She was gone, and yet she was still everywhere—in the pulse of every star, in the whisper of the wind, in the silence that stretched endlessly above him. Her love remained woven into the very fabric of the universe.

Lior stood at the edge of the tower, gazing out into the cosmos, the cold wind tugging at his cloak. The light of distant stars illuminated the night, casting long shadows on the ground, their brilliance so steady, so constant. But even their light could not banish the darkness that threatened to rise again.

The darkness had not disappeared. No, it had simply receded into the farthest reaches of the universe, waiting for its next opportunity to strike. He could feel it, like a distant thunderstorm, just beyond the horizon. There were cracks in the fabric of the stars, slight but real, and Lior knew they would not hold forever. The balance they had fought for—this fragile peace—would one day be tested again. It always was.

But Lior had made a vow. A vow to Isolde. He would protect the stars for as long as they burned, for as long as his heart still beat. He would fight the darkness whenever it came, knowing that it was his duty to guard the light that had been restored— his duty to honor the love that had saved the universe.

"I will never stop," he whispered into the wind, his voice quiet against the vastness of the night. "I will never stop watching over you."

The stars shimmered in response, as if the very universe were listening, acknowledging his words. But the stillness around him was thick, heavy with the weight of unspoken truths. He could feel the presence of something out there, just beyond the veil of the stars, something that watched and waited.

It was always like this now. The feeling of being watched. The knowledge that darkness still lingered, lurking in the corners of existence, waiting for a crack in the walls that protected the light. There had been a time when he had felt secure—when Isolde's sacrifice had given him the strength to carry on, when their bond had been the only thing that mattered. But now, even the stars seemed to tremble under the weight of what was to come.

Lior's eyes narrowed as his gaze swept across the sky. His thoughts were interrupted by the faintest sound, the softest whisper that carried through the wind. It was a voice, not his own, and it sent a shiver down his spine. He knew that voice.

Lior...

His heart raced. The stars around him seemed to shimmer in response, their light shifting, as if acknowledging the presence of the one he could never forget.

Isolde...

The whisper was faint, barely audible, yet so clear in his mind that it felt as though she were standing right beside him. He inhaled sharply, his breath catching in his throat, and for a brief moment, he allowed himself to believe. He allowed himself to feel the presence of her love, to feel the warmth of her soul, once again.

I am with you, always.

Lior closed his eyes, feeling the pull of her words, the pulse of her love reverberating through his very being. She was always with him. In the stars, in the wind, in the very fabric of the universe that surrounded him. Her love was a part of him, and as long as the stars burned, it would always be.

But even as the warmth of her love filled him, the cold reality of his duties crept back in. He could not remain lost in the memory of her. He had a role to play, a responsibility that could not be neglected.

You must protect them, Lior. Protect the stars. Protect the universe. Isolde's voice was softer now, fading, but still present. *Our love will guide you. Always.*

Lior nodded, though she could not see him. He knew what he had to do. He had known it since the moment she had made her sacrifice. He had known that his work was far from over. The universe was still at risk, and while the stars may have been reborn, there would always be forces that would seek to corrupt them, to consume them.

He opened his eyes, and the vastness of the cosmos stretched before him, both beautiful and terrifying. The stars were steady, their light unwavering, but there was a crack in the sky. A rift, barely visible, but enough to catch his attention. Something was stirring out there—something ancient and hungry.

His fingers tightened around the edge of the tower as he gazed into the distance, the chill of the night air biting at his skin. He could feel it—the pulse of the darkness, just beyond his reach. The calm before the storm.

I will not let it happen again, Lior thought, his voice steady in the silence. *I will protect the stars. And I will protect you, Isolde. Forever.*

The wind swept through him again, pulling at his cloak, and he could almost hear her voice once more, a whisper on the breeze.

Forever...

With a final glance at the stars above, Lior turned and walked toward the inner sanctum of the tower. His footsteps were steady, resolute, his mind focused on the task ahead. The universe had been reborn, but it was not without its flaws. Darkness would always seek to rise, always seek to corrupt. And as long as he was the guardian of the stars, he would stand between them and that darkness.

He entered the heart of the tower, where the shimmering Heart of the Universe stood, pulsing with the energy of the stars. The glowing crystal at its center hummed softly, like the beating of a heart, echoing through the vast chamber. This was where the stars had been created, where their destinies had been woven. And it was here that Lior would come to learn, to understand, and to keep the stars safe.

He reached out, placing his hand on the heart, feeling the steady pulse of energy flow through him. The warmth of the stars filled him, filling the empty space where his grief had once been. This was his purpose—this was his life now. The universe had been given to him, entrusted to him. And he would not fail.

But even as he stood there, the universe began to tremble, ever so slightly, as though it, too, was waiting for something.

A crack, barely perceptible, appeared at the edge of the star-filled sky. It was just a shimmer, a ripple of darkness against the shimmering light, but it was enough to catch his attention. The stars flickered, their light wavering, and a chill ran down his spine.

Lior's hand tightened on the heart, his gaze fixed on the darkness that seemed to spread slowly across the sky. The balance was fragile, as it always had been. And this time, there would be no sacrifice to save them. This time, it would be up to him.

The wind outside howled, the darkness creeping ever closer,

as if it could sense his resolve.

The final battle had not yet come—but it was drawing near. And Lior, now more than ever, could feel it.

The universe was shifting, the stars were flickering, and something ancient—something insidious—was rising again.

Lior clenched his fists, his jaw set with determination. The End of Eternity had not yet arrived.

But it was coming.

And when it did, he would stand ready. The stars would burn brighter than ever before, and he would protect them. No matter the cost.

The tremor in the air grew more pronounced, vibrating deep within the walls of the tower. Lior could feel it in the very marrow of his bones—the darkness that stirred beyond the veil, spreading outward from the cracks in the sky. It wasn't merely a whisper now. It was a growing storm, one that threatened to break through the fragile peace the universe had managed to hold onto.

He stood at the Heart of the Universe, his hand still pressed against the glowing crystal, feeling its pulse—a slow, steady rhythm, like the heartbeat of the cosmos itself. But even the Heart was beginning to falter, its glow dimming just slightly, as if it, too, could sense the gathering threat. The stars outside flickered as well, their light becoming more erratic, their steady pulse disturbed by something unseen, something creeping in from the edges.

Isolde... Lior thought, his heart aching at the thought of her. The bond they had shared, the love that had transcended time and space, was the very thing that had saved the stars. It was her sacrifice that had restored balance, and now, he stood alone, shouldering the weight of the universe's fate.

But the darkness—he could feel it. It was closer now. The stars were dimming. The balance was teetering on the edge.

He drew in a deep breath, his chest tightening as the urgency of the moment pressed down on him. The weight of his duty, the burden of the stars, was heavier than ever. Isolde's voice—soft, distant, but undeniably present—echoed in the back of his mind.

You are never alone, Lior. Not even when the stars flicker or the darkness rises. Our love will guide you through the storm.

Her words, as faint as they were, steadied him. They filled the empty space that threatened to overwhelm him, and for a moment, he could feel her beside him once again—her love, her presence, like the warmth of the stars themselves.

He turned away from the Heart, a quiet resolve settling in his chest. His role as the guardian of the stars was never meant to be easy. It had always been a responsibility, a calling that would test him in ways he couldn't even begin to understand. But now, as he stood on the precipice of a new threat, he understood more clearly than ever before that this was not just about protecting the stars. It was about preserving the love that had shaped them, the love that had saved them, and ensuring that it would never fade.

The stars had been born from the light of that love. And though darkness would always rise to challenge the light, Lior knew one thing for certain: the love between him and Isolde would never die. It was eternal. And as long as the stars burned, as long as the Heart of the Universe pulsed with energy, that love would burn bright, too.

He stepped away from the Heart, his footsteps echoing through the hollow, vast chamber. The stillness of the tower seemed to close in around him, the weight of what was to come pressing down with an undeniable urgency.

As he left the chamber, he moved swiftly through the corridors, each step bringing him closer to the towering windows of the celestial hall. The sky outside had darkened further, a swirling mass of deep blue and black, with streaks of silver and gold cutting through the darkness. The stars, though still burning brightly, were dimmer now, their light flickering in rhythmic pulses. There was a disturbance in the air—an almost palpable tension that gripped the universe like a tightening noose.

Lior stepped out onto the balcony that overlooked the vast expanse of the cosmos. The wind howled again, louder this time, and it carried with it a strange, unfamiliar scent—something old, something ancient. His instincts flared, and his eyes narrowed as he scanned the sky. The stars, once steady in their glow, were now flickering more rapidly, their light growing more unstable with every passing moment.

His breath caught in his throat as his gaze locked onto the source of the disturbance. A dark shadow was creeping through the stars, moving faster than it should have, as though it were eating through the very fabric of the universe. The darkness was spreading, blotting out the stars in its wake. And in the center of it all, something—someone—was controlling it. Lior could feel its power, a sinister force that surged with malevolent intent.

For the first time in months, a cold chill of fear gripped him. The shadows had returned.

The stars seemed to pulse again, as though calling out to him, warning him of the danger that loomed. The warmth of Isolde's love, still ever-present, seemed to flicker with a renewed intensity. *You are not alone, Lior,* her voice whispered once again, and he clung to it like a lifeline. *You have the strength to face this.*

The darkness ahead shifted, twisting and turning in unnatural shapes. Lior's instincts screamed at him to act. His hand tightened around the hilt of his sword, and for a brief moment, he could feel the weight of his role as guardian. He had been prepared for this—had known that one day, the balance would be tested again. But even now, with the stars dimming and the shadows closing in, he could not escape the deep, gnawing fear in his chest.

Isolde's love is with me, Lior reminded himself, his voice quiet but firm in his mind. *It is in the stars. It is in me.*

He squared his shoulders, his gaze never leaving the encroaching darkness. The universe was vast, and its forces—both light and dark—were beyond his full comprehension. But one thing was clear: he would protect the stars, no matter the cost.

The darkness surged forward, now clearly visible as a swirling mass of inky blackness that consumed everything in its path. It was more than just shadow. It was alive—alive in a way that was unnatural, as though it had its own purpose, its own hunger.

Lior stepped forward, drawing his sword in one fluid motion. The blade gleamed in the dimming light, reflecting the last of the stars' glow. He could feel the energy of the stars flowing through him, their power strengthening him, but it wasn't enough to hold back the darkness. Not yet.

The wind picked up again, howling around him, carrying with it the whispers of the stars. *Fight, Lior. You have the power of love, of light, of the universe itself. Do not let the darkness consume it.*

Lior's heart raced as the shadows closed in, but his resolve was unwavering. He would not allow Isolde's sacrifice to be in vain. He would protect the stars, and he would protect the love they had shared.

With a deep breath, he stepped forward, his sword raised, ready to face the darkness. It would not take the stars. It would not take Isolde's legacy.

Not if he could help it.

The universe trembled around him as the shadow surged toward him, and for a moment, Lior felt himself pulled into the swirling abyss of darkness. He could feel it—it was everywhere, an endless void that threatened to swallow him whole. But just as the darkness closed in, something inside of him flared— an energy, a force, a light that was brighter than the stars themselves.

Isolde's love.

He clung to it, with all his strength, and the universe seemed to respond. The stars flared to life, their light pulsing, filling the vast expanse with a brilliance that pushed back against the encroaching shadow. The darkness recoiled, but it was not enough. The battle between light and dark would not be won so easily.

Lior raised his sword high, the energy of the stars flowing through him, and in that moment, he understood what it meant to be the guardian. To protect the stars, to protect the love that had been born from them, he had to stand against the darkness—not just for the stars, but for everything that came after. For the balance of the universe. For Isolde.

The wind howled, and the light of the stars burned brighter, stronger than it had ever been before.

The darkness trembled.

And Lior knew, in that moment, that he was ready to fight. To protect the stars. To protect her. Forever.

Between the Ember and the Tide

The winds had shifted.

Lior stood at the highest point of the celestial tower, his silhouette framed against the expanse of a sky that had long since stopped being just a backdrop to his existence. Now, the universe—the infinite sea of stars, galaxies, and cosmic wonders—was a part of him. The fabric of the stars, once distant, once so cold and far, now flowed in his veins. He could feel the pulse of each light, the hum of each planet, the whisper of each celestial being.

But the peace he had fought for—fought with his heart, with his very soul—had come at a price. The universe had been restored, yes, but at the cost of something far more profound than even the stars themselves.

Isolde was gone, not in body, but in spirit—her essence woven into the stars. Their love, once tangible, once physical, now existed in the wind, in the flickering of the stars, in the soft hum of the universe. Their bond had transcended the limits of the physical realm, leaving behind a legacy, a myth, a whisper.

And yet, Lior could still feel her.

The wind stirred around him, carrying with it the faintest echo of her voice. *Lior...* It was soft, like a memory too sweet to touch, yet so real, so vivid that he could almost hear her beside him. Her love was embedded in the stars, in the very air that swirled around him, but it was more than that. It was alive in the rhythm of the universe itself, in every flicker of light, in the flow of time, in the beating of his heart.

The silence of the universe was loud. The calm before the storm of time itself, before the next trial of the stars. For even as the galaxies spun in their age-old dance, even as the celestial balance rested in the delicate equilibrium forged by Isolde's sacrifice, there was an undeniable sense of tension, a warning that drifted on the cosmic winds.

Something was coming.

Lior's eyes narrowed as he gazed across the vastness of space, the stars now burning steadily, their light filling the universe with warmth, with life. Yet, as beautiful as the stars were, they could not mask the darkness that lay beyond. It was an ever-present force, waiting for an opening, waiting for a moment of weakness. Just as love could heal and bind, so too could darkness consume and tear apart.

And in the silence of the universe, Lior could feel it—the stirrings of something ancient, something that had never been truly vanquished. The darkness.

It had not been defeated when Isolde gave her life for the stars. It had only been sealed. And Lior, now the guardian of the stars, knew that his duty was not over. The stars would continue to burn, but he was the keeper of their light. The universe had been changed, irrevocably, but he could not rest. Not yet.

A faint rustle behind him made Lior turn, his hand instinctively reaching for the sword at his side. But there was no threat. Just the soft movement of the air, the whisper of the wind.

Lior, don't be afraid.

Her voice. This time, it was more distinct, a melody that reached out to him from across the veil of existence. He closed his eyes, letting the warmth of her love wash over him like the sun's first light after a storm.

I will always be with you.

Lior's breath hitched as he stood there, alone on the precipice of the universe, surrounded by the endless expanse of stars, feeling the weight of her words. Her love had saved him, had given him the strength to protect the stars, to guard the balance. She had given everything, and he had vowed to carry on her legacy.

But even the stars had a time. Even the stars could flicker, could fade.

A faint rumbling began, a tremor that vibrated through the tower, through the ground beneath his feet. He felt it deep in his chest, an unsettling vibration, a foreboding force stirring in the distant reaches of space. His heart quickened as he looked up at the stars, watching as their light flickered for just a moment, the calm steady pulse interrupted by a faint, sudden shift in the air.

Lior stepped forward, moving with purpose, knowing that whatever was coming, it was inevitable. He had stood at the edge of the universe before, and he would do so again. But this time, it felt different. The shadows that had once lingered at the edges of existence were no longer distant whispers. They were closing in.

It is not over, Lior. Isolde's voice was more urgent now, the familiar warmth of her love tinged with an undercurrent of something darker. *You must be ready.*

He didn't need to ask her what she meant. He could feel it— the pulse of the darkness, the ebb and flow of cosmic energy that trembled in the air. It was a threat that had always been there, lurking, waiting. A force that would challenge the light, that would always challenge the balance between good and evil, fire and water, light and dark.

The stars above him flickered again, a rapid stuttering of their once steady light, and the air around him grew still. The wind ceased, and for a moment, Lior could hear only his own heartbeat. Time seemed to stretch, the silence so thick, so heavy, that he thought for a moment he might suffocate in it.

Then, a crackle of energy split the stillness. The stars flared violently, their light pulsing in a frantic rhythm, as though they were being torn apart by an unseen force. A shadow— long, slithering, crawling from the edge of space—moved with a speed that defied nature. It spread out across the sky like ink in water, spreading its tendrils across the stars. The once steady rhythm of the universe was thrown into chaos.

Lior...

The voice came again, faint, yet louder now. It was Isolde's voice, reaching out to him through the rift, through the darkening cosmos. He could feel her fear. She was still with him, still alive in the stars, but something had changed. Something had broken through the barrier.

Do not let them win, Lior. Her words were urgent, but there was no time for fear. There was only time for action.

With a rush of adrenaline, Lior turned, his sword drawn in a fluid motion. His gaze fixed on the stars, his heart beating faster as the pulse of dark energy seemed to come from every direction. He could feel the pressure—an overwhelming, suffocating weight that pressed against him from all sides.

It was a force beyond anything he had ever faced. A force that threatened not only the stars but everything. Time itself seemed to stretch and buckle under the weight of the shadows. The fabric of reality was unraveling, the delicate threads of life and death, light and dark, beginning to fray.

The first sign of the attack came from above. A bolt of black lightning tore through the sky, crashing down with a force that shook the tower to its very core. The stars dimmed, their brilliance flickering out one by one as if their light were being drained, sucked into the void that was expanding before him.

Lior's heart raced. This was it. The moment he had feared. The moment when darkness would rise again, when the very stars would flicker and die. He had to act.

He raised his sword high, feeling the pulse of the stars flow through him once again, their energy still within his grasp. But the darkness was stronger now, pressing against him like a living thing, as if it knew his every move before he made it.

Lior...

The wind carried her voice again, but this time it wasn't just a whisper—it was a command. *You are not alone. Stand firm, my love. You will not let them fall.*

He clenched his jaw, his grip tightening on the sword. The stars—his stars, their stars—had been born from the light of their love. And no darkness, no force in the universe, would take that away.

The universe trembled as the darkness surged forward, but Lior's resolve burned bright. The stars would not fall. Not while he still stood.

He surged forward, meeting the shadow head-on, his sword cutting through the air with a fierce clarity. As he swung, the light of the stars burst forth from the blade, clashing against the dark, illuminating the vast sky. The battle had begun, and this time, Lior would not let the darkness win.

He would stand. He would fight. And he would protect the stars—*their* stars—forever.

The clash between light and darkness was more than just a battle of wills—it was the very essence of existence, the force that held the universe together. Lior's sword sliced through the air with a brilliant flash, the stars within its blade shimmering in response to his unyielding determination. The darkness recoiled, but it didn't retreat. It swarmed, a liquid shadow that pulsed and writhed, ever encroaching, ever hungry.

The sky above him trembled, the once-sturdy stars flickering in distress as the dark energy bled through the fabric of the universe. The stars—their light, their essence—was being siphoned away, pulled into the yawning blackness like moths drawn to a flame. Each flicker was a wound on the universe itself, and Lior could feel it in his soul.

I won't let this happen, he thought, his chest tight with the fear and fury of what was unfolding. *The stars will never fade.*

Isolde's voice echoed in his mind, as if to calm his racing thoughts, to steady him as the storm raged around him. *You are the light, Lior. You are the guardian. Let the stars guide you.*

The words were a beacon in the storm, and Lior drew strength from them. He squared his shoulders and pressed forward, his feet moving with a certainty born from the deepest part of his soul. The stars in his blade burned brighter, their light slicing through the darkness, and with every step, the shadow recoiled.

But the shadow was relentless. It surged again, this time with a force that shook the very stars themselves. Lior staggered back, the weight of the force pushing him off balance, but he didn't fall. He couldn't afford to.

The wind around him howled, sharp and biting. The once gentle breeze, carrying whispers of Isolde's love, was now filled with an ominous charge—electric and unstable. The sky overhead twisted, the stars blinking out one by one, swallowed by the darkness. It was as if the world itself was holding its breath, suspended between light and shadow.

Lior's heart pounded in his chest as he looked up, desperate to find a way to restore the balance, to push back the force that threatened to destroy everything they had fought for. He felt the warmth of the stars growing colder, the once-steady pulse of their light becoming erratic, as though even the stars themselves were losing their strength.

Isolde... he thought, his voice a silent prayer. *Please. Give me strength.*

The darkness answered with a violent surge. Tendrils of shadow reached out, lashing at him like serpents, trying to wrap around him, trying to suffocate the light. Lior swung his sword again, the blade crackling with starfire, but the shadows twisted, adapting, pushing back against him.

Then, just as it seemed the darkness might swallow him whole, a new force surged in the air—a familiar, powerful presence, the pulse of a force that only he could feel.

Lior.

It was her voice, unmistakable, ringing through him like a song carried on the wind. Her love flooded through him, a fierce warmth that cut through the chill of the darkness.

I am with you.

He felt the stars flare, their light burning brighter, their pulse steady again, as though they had heard her words too. As though the very stars had become part of her, and she, in turn, had become part of them. Lior raised his sword high once more, his gaze fixed on the shadow before him.

We are the light, he thought, his voice echoing in the vastness of the universe. *And the light will not falter.*

The darkness before him shrieked, its tendrils recoiling from the pure light now flowing through him. Lior focused all of his energy, channeling the strength of the stars, of his love for Isolde, and the force that had been gathering within him surged outward, a wave of radiance that tore through the dark like a burning comet.

The universe trembled, the cosmic energy pulsing, as the light grew brighter, engulfing everything in its path. The darkness fought, resisted, but it was no match for the sheer force of Lior's will. The shadows that had once felt invincible now shrank back, unable to withstand the force of the stars, of love itself.

And then, as quickly as it had come, the darkness began to dissipate, fading into the ether, retreating back into the void from which it had emerged. The stars that had once flickered and dimmed now burned bright again, steady and unwavering in the vast expanse of the universe.

Lior stood there, panting, his body trembling with the effort, but the weight of the battle had lifted. The stars were safe once more. The balance had been restored. The shadow was gone.

For now.

Lior lowered his sword, the last remnants of darkness fading from the blade. The wind around him softened, and the stars above seemed to sigh in relief, their light steady and warm once more. But even as the calm settled in, Lior knew this wasn't the end. Darkness would always return. It always did. But he was ready.

Isolde's presence lingered, filling him with the quiet certainty that her love would always guide him. They had won this battle, but the war for the stars would never truly end.

But they had time. Time to fight, to love, and to protect.

Lior closed his eyes, taking a deep breath, feeling the weight of the universe settling around him. He could feel her in every flicker of light, in every breath of wind, in every pulse of the stars. Isolde was with him, always.

And as long as the stars burned, as long as the universe continued to unfold, their love would live on—forever.

He gazed up at the heavens, the stars burning steady, their light illuminating the infinite sky. Their love had saved the universe, and it would continue to protect it, even when darkness threatened.

Lior stood tall, the weight of his role as the guardian no longer a burden but a privilege. The stars were safe. The balance had been restored. And he would keep it that way.

We are the light, Lior thought again, the words as much a promise as a prayer.

And the light would never fade.

Twenty

Forever Bound

The universe was still.

The stars above shimmered as if they had always been there, eternal and untouchable. Their light cut through the infinite blackness, casting a pale glow over the vast expanse of space. Time seemed to hold its breath, as though the world itself paused in awe of what had just transpired. The ripples of darkness had subsided, but in their wake, something had changed—something profound.

Lior stood alone, his feet planted firmly on the soft earth of the celestial realm, his heart heavy, yet full of a strange, aching peace. The sword in his hand was cool now, the flames of the battle having long since extinguished. He had fought for the stars, fought for the balance, and now, he stood in silence, watching as the universe adjusted to the calm. But this calm was different. It wasn't the same stillness he had felt before, when he had been trapped in his duty and the weight of the stars. Now, it was something new—something that spoke of endings and new beginnings, of love that transcended time and space.

The stars flickered once, then grew brighter, their light pulsing in a rhythm that felt like a heartbeat—steady, strong, and resolute. It was as if they were alive, as if they too were aware of the great change that had taken place. And somewhere, in the deep recesses of his soul, Lior knew why.

Isolde.

Her presence washed over him like a tide, gentle and eternal. Her love, though no longer physical, had never left him. It was woven into the very fabric of the cosmos. It was in every flicker of light, every soft wind that brushed against his face, every beat of his heart. It was as if she had become one with the stars, her spirit, her essence, woven into the universe she had saved.

He closed his eyes, his hand resting lightly against his chest, as if he could hold her love in his palm. The memories of her— the sound of her laughter, the warmth of her touch, the fire of their passion, and the quiet moments they shared—rushed over him like the ebb and flow of the tide. Her love was still with him, more powerful now than it had ever been.

Lior...

Her voice was soft, like the faintest whisper of wind through the trees, but it was enough. Enough to fill his heart, enough to remind him of all that they had sacrificed and all that they had gained. Their love was not just a memory. It was a force, an energy that lived on in the stars, in the universe, in the very light that shone from every corner of existence.

Isolde... he whispered into the quiet night, his voice thick with emotion. *I'm here.*

The wind around him shifted, gently caressing his face, as though answering him, as though she were with him in that moment. He could almost feel the warmth of her presence beside him, the steady rhythm of her heartbeat echoing in the stars.

We are bound, Lior, her voice came again, clearer now, stronger. *Forever.*

And in that moment, Lior understood.

The love they had shared was no longer bound by time, nor by death. It had become a part of the very fabric of the universe—intertwined with the stars, with the light, with everything. Isolde had given herself to the stars, to the cosmos, but in doing so, she had left a part of herself with him. A part that could never be severed, a part that would always guide him.

He looked up at the sky, his eyes drawn to the First Constellation—the constellation they had both loved, the one that had borne witness to their love, to their sacrifice. It burned brighter than ever, its stars a constant reminder of what they had accomplished, of what they had built. Their love was immortalized in its light, forever burning, forever guiding.

The world around him seemed to shift. The stars seemed to swell, growing brighter, as if they were moving closer to him, reaching out to touch him, to connect with him. And in that moment, Lior felt the full force of Isolde's love—an energy that surged through him, filling him with a warmth that radiated from his very soul. He was no longer just Lior, the guardian of the stars. He was a part of the stars, a part of Isolde's love.

The stars pulsed in the sky, their light growing in intensity, as if they, too, were acknowledging the bond they shared. It was as though the entire universe had come to life, its heart beating in rhythm with his own. The balance, which had once been so fragile, now felt unbreakable. The stars had been reborn, but now they had become something more—something eternal. They were a testament to the love that had saved them, to the bond that had never truly broken.

Lior closed his eyes again, his breath steady, as he allowed the warmth of Isolde's presence to fill him. He could feel the stars within him, their light burning brightly, their energy flowing through him. She was with him—always.

The universe will never forget us, Isolde's voice whispered, her words a caress against his heart. *We will live on in every flicker of light, in every pulse of the stars. Our love will guide the universe, as the stars guide the night.*

A smile tugged at Lior's lips, his heart swelling with a quiet, profound joy. He had given everything—his heart, his soul, his very existence—to protect the stars. And in doing so, he had ensured that their love would never die. Isolde had given herself to the stars, but in doing so, she had given them both a new kind of immortality. Their love would never fade. It would never be forgotten. It would live on, eternally, in the hearts of those who came after them.

The world around him seemed to hold its breath as he stood there, bathed in the light of the stars, the very air vibrating with the energy of the cosmos. The stars above him shone brighter, their light pulsing in perfect harmony with his own heartbeat. Every star, every flicker of light, was a part of them. Their legacy was forever woven into the fabric of the universe.

And in that moment, Lior knew the truth—there was no end. Not for their love. Not for the stars.

The stars would burn for eternity, and so would their love.

He turned, his gaze drifting over the vast landscape, the entire universe laid out before him. The winds stirred again, carrying with them the distant echoes of Isolde's laughter, the gentle whisper of her voice.

I am always with you, Lior. Forever.

A sense of peace settled over him, and he knew, deep in his heart, that this was the beginning of something new. The universe would continue to unfold, the stars would continue to burn, and their love would guide it all. It would be a beacon of hope for every soul who looked up at the sky, a reminder that love—true, unbreakable love—had the power to save the universe.

Lior smiled softly, the weight of the universe settling comfortably on his shoulders. He had been given a second chance. A chance to protect the stars, to honor the memory of the woman he loved, and to carry their love forward, forever bound between the ember and the tide.

The stars shimmered above him, burning brighter than ever, their light eternal. And in that light, he could feel her—always.

Forever.

Lior stood still, bathed in the shimmering glow of the stars, his heart filled with the weight of eternity. The wind whispered softly around him, as if carrying the voices of the universe itself—so many echoes, so many stories, woven together across the ages. Isolde's presence was everywhere, in every spark of light, in the steady rhythm of the stars' pulse.

His hand, once trembling with the burden of the stars, was now steady. He had walked through darkness and light, through loss and rebirth. He had given everything for the stars, and in return, the universe had given him something far more precious than he had ever expected: Isolde's love, woven into the very fabric of existence. It was a love that transcended time, space, and even death itself. A love that would never fade.

The stars above him grew brighter as if acknowledging his thoughts, their light spreading out across the universe, illuminating the vast expanse. Each flicker, each pulse, was a reminder that their love had saved them all. The cosmic dance of fire and water, light and dark, was not just a battle—it was a beautiful, eternal balance. And he had been a part of it.

Lior felt the stirring of a new understanding, a deep connection to the universe that went beyond the roles of guardian and protector. He had once believed that his duty was solely to protect the stars, to keep them from falling into darkness. But now, as he stood there, watching the night unfold before him, he realized that his purpose was so much more. He was part of something greater—something eternal. He was a part of the love that had saved the universe, and that love would continue to guide him, to guide everyone, for as long as the stars burned.

As the stars shone brightly above, Lior took a slow step forward, the weight of his responsibilities settling into his soul with a newfound clarity. Every day, he had fought to keep the balance intact. And now, with Isolde's love pulsing through him, he knew that his fight had not been in vain. He would continue to protect the stars, not just for the universe, but for her—for the love they had shared.

The wind shifted again, warmer this time, carrying the scent of the earth and the distant sound of rustling leaves. It was as if the world itself was waking up, stretching, taking in the peace that had settled over it. Lior's gaze drifted to the First Constellation—their constellation—the one they had always cherished. Its light burned brighter than ever before, a testament to their love, to the sacrifice they had both made. It was as though their love had become one with the stars, and every flicker of light, every pulse of energy, was a reflection of that bond.

Lior could feel her, feel her presence in the stars, in the breeze, in the steady hum of the universe. She was with him—always. And in that moment, he realized something that filled him with an overwhelming sense of peace.

Their love would never die. It could not die. It had become a part of the universe itself, woven into every star, every galaxy, every breath of wind. It was immortal, eternal, just as the stars were.

He turned from the balcony and walked back into the heart of the celestial tower. His steps were calm, measured. But beneath that calm, beneath the steady pace of his feet on the ground, his heart was soaring. His love for Isolde had not ended. It had transformed, had transcended into something greater, something beyond what either of them could have imagined.

In the silence of the tower, Lior stood in front of the Heart of the Universe, the shimmering crystal at its center pulsing with the energy of the stars. He placed his hand gently on its surface, feeling the familiar warmth beneath his fingertips. This was where everything had begun—where their love had taken root and where it had grown, blooming into the force that had saved the stars.

He closed his eyes, feeling the power of the Heart flow through him, the stars and the universe filling him with their steady pulse. The universe had been born from the light of the stars. But now, it was different. Now, the universe was a reflection of his love for Isolde. A love that could never fade, a love that would continue to protect the stars, to guide them, and to keep them burning bright.

And as Lior stood there, with the Heart of the Universe in his hands, he knew that their love had become something more than a fleeting moment in time. It had become part of the very fabric of existence. The universe would continue, as it always had, but it would do so with a new understanding of what truly mattered. Light, love, sacrifice—these things were eternal. They were the very essence of the stars.

The wind outside shifted again, carrying with it the faintest whisper of Isolde's voice. *You have done it, Lior. You have saved them. You have saved us. You have saved the universe.*

Her voice, though soft, resonated with an undeniable strength. And in that moment, Lior knew that her love, their love, would live on in every star, in every flicker of light, forever.

He smiled, a peaceful expression settling over his features, and then, with one final glance at the stars above, he turned away from the balcony. His duties as the guardian would never end, but he no longer felt the weight of them as a burden. They were a gift—a chance to protect what mattered most. The love that had saved the universe. The love that would never die.

As Lior walked deeper into the heart of the tower, the wind carrying the faintest traces of Isolde's voice, he knew one thing with certainty: the stars would always burn bright. And their love would always be there—forever, between the ember and the tide.

The End.

www.ingramcontent.com/pod-product-compliance
Lightning Source LLC
Chambersburg PA
CBHW051100050726
47592CB00002B/604